LIVING
ABOVE THE BAR

Also by Dr. Emerson Eggerichs

Love & Respect
Mother & Son
Love & Respect in The Family
The 4 Wills of God
The Love & Respect Experience
Speak Your Mind

LIVING
ABOVE THE BAR

12 Qualities That Win Hearts,
Influence Lives, and Appeal to the World

Dr. Emerson Eggerichs

PUNCHLINE
PUBLISHERS

PUNCHLINE PUBLISHERS

Living Above the Bar
Copyright © 2024 by Dr. Emerson Eggerichs
First paperback edition October 2024

ISBN 978-1-955051-41-5 (Paperback)
ISBN 978-1-955051-42-2 (eBook)

Cover and interior design: Heather Seeger

The author is represented by Joy Eggerichs Reed of Punchline Agency
www.punchlineagency.com

Dedication

Having pastored East Lansing Trinity Church in Michigan from 1980 to 1999, I wish to dedicate this book to the many who modeled living above the bar. The Lansing area uniquely consisted of the Capitol of Michigan, the Oldsmobile plant for car production, and Michigan State University—politics, commerce, and education converging in one city. In those environments, I observed firsthand the quality of life many Christians in my congregation brought to those settings. They were in the governor's office and legislature, serving with integrity and compassion; in senior management at the auto plant, leading with diligence and fairness; and in academia as deans and world-renowned researchers, exemplifying excellence and humility. Many also held support staff positions in these environments, doing so with distinction. Their unwavering faith and commitment to Christ influenced these diverse arenas, demonstrating what it means to live out one's beliefs boldly and faithfully, no matter the sphere of influence. This book is a tribute to their dedication, courage, and the light they shone in every corner of our community. Some keep striving to have *done well*, while others have finished the race and heard, "Well done."

Table of Contents

Letter From Emerson

Why have I written this book now? Those who know me associate my work often with the themes of my first book, *Love & Respect*, which is on the topic of marriage and rooted in the truth of Ephesians 5:33. I aimed to simply and succinctly quote the Scripture on love and respect and offer practical applications for those in the congregation wanting a Christ-centered marriage. As a senior pastor for twenty years, my job every Sunday was to share what I found in the Bible and help the people in my community understand the teaching in ways that applied to their lives. The traction from the specific *Love & Respect* message exceeded anything I could have imagined, and my wife Sarah and I have been teaching and serving through our Love and Respect ministry full-time since 1999.

However, since I will never stop studying God's Word or having a pastoral perspective beyond just the topic of marriage, I continue to observe the world around me and what God's Word would say to Christians today. One theme that continues to come to mind as I study is: Living Above the Bar!

- **1 Peter 2:12:** "Keep your behavior excellent among the Gentiles, so that in the thing in which they slander you as evildoers, they may, because of your good deeds, as they observe them, glorify God on the day of visitation."

- **1 Peter 3:16:** "Keep a good conscience so that in the thing in which you are slandered, those who disparage your good behavior in Christ will be put to shame."

One primary area where I see the idea of "Living Above the Bar" really unraveling for many of us is **politics.**

Perhaps you've picked this book up because, as an American, we have just gone through a very intense presidential election. Maybe your candidate won, and you are rejoicing. Maybe your candidate lost, and you are devastated and fearful of the future. I wrote this book to help you navigate and utilize what Scripture says about how we should participate as citizens, stand up for what we believe, and respond in our everyday lives to help us live…above the bar.

So, let me address how we can live above the bar in politics first…

Peter urges Christians to maintain excellent behavior and a clear conscience, embodying moral integrity and uprightness even when facing slander or false accusations. In today's polarized society, where social and political divisions are inevitable, navigating these tensions while remaining true to our faith is particularly challenging. Peter's letters provide invaluable guidance on how to conduct ourselves amid fear, criticism, or opposition.

He emphasizes that our good deeds and consistent testimony, even in times of discord, can serve as a powerful witness. By standing firm in our convictions with grace and humility, we vindicate ourselves before God and others and create opportunities for even those who oppose us to acknowledge the goodness of our actions and ultimately glorify God.

This book will cover twelve different areas I want to encourage and equip you in as a Believer to win hearts, influence lives, and appeal to the world—to live above the bar. I have received hundreds of thousands of emails, messages, comments, and in-person anecdotes since starting Love and Respect, and many shared how a message or point encouraged a reader or audience member to change something to be more like Christ. Many of these testimonies are shared throughout these pages as they relate to the topic being discussed. They are a powerful demonstration of how our everyday lives can be changed when we change our approach to even the most minute areas of our lives.

Peter calls for Christians to live above reproach, reflecting Christ's light in all circumstances so that even those disparaging us are left with no grounds to accuse. As we strive to live by God's standards, we bear witness to His truth, leading others to recognize His presence in our lives and reconsider their judgments. Our lives should be a testimony that inspire non-believers and fellow believers, showing kindness and humility, speaking truth with love, and seeking connection over conflict. This witness can lead others to retract their disparaging words and glorify God.

The world inherently understands what is right. Paul expressed this clearly when he wrote, "For we are taking pains to do what is right, not only in the eyes of the Lord but also in the eyes of man" (2 Corinthians 8:21). The world watches us closely and recognizes when we act rightly because they, too, know what is right. Therefore, we must strive to uphold what is right before God and others.

Remember, God has written His law on every human heart. Paul explains in Romans 2:14-15, "Indeed, when Gentiles, who do not have the law, do by nature things required by the law... They show that the requirements of the law are written on their hearts." In other words, though people may lie, steal, and cheat, they still know it is wrong because they do not want anyone to lie to them, steal from them, or cheat against them. Christians and non-Christians alike know what good behaviors are.

As Jesus taught in Matthew 7:12 (NIV): "So in everything, do to others what you would have them do to you, for this sums up the Law and the Prophets." Similarly, Luke 6:31 (NIV) says, "Do to others as you would have them do to you."

My friend Sam Ericsson, who graduated from Harvard Law School and helped draft new constitutions for key nations during the collapse of the Soviet Union, would often be asked how to create just laws. He would reply, "The Golden Rule: Do to others what you want them to do for you if you were in their situation. If you were a minority, how would you want to be treated legally?" Every legislator understood this perfectly. Sam shared with me that the struggle wasn't with the inherent rightness of the Golden Rule but with overcoming their prejudices. The challenge lay not in comprehending the principle but in applying it fairly.

This is the crux of why our conduct as believers is so crucial. When we embody the principles of love, respect, and integrity, we testify to a higher standard—God's standard. Our actions become a reflection of Christ Himself, illuminating the moral and ethical truths that resonate in every human heart. When we act with kindness, fairness, and honesty, we not only uphold the values that the world recognizes as good but also point to the source of those values—God's truth. This living witness can soften hearts and open minds, even in the most contentious and polarized environments.

As followers of Christ, our call is not just to win arguments or debates, but to win hearts. What we speak with conviction is vital, but if our lives don't embody the truth we proclaim, our words will fall on deaf ears.

But should we aim to share our beliefs and engage in debates in this political climate? Absolutely. We are a people of moral and Biblical conviction. When Sarah and I pray during a political season, we refuse to adopt the attitude of "Let's agree to disagree." We must do everything within our legal rights to communicate what we believe is wrong, especially when it's on the legislative agenda, and vote accordingly. This is a matter of policy, and it has deep moral significance.

During one election in my younger days, I voted for a candidate primarily because he openly professed to be a born-again Christian. At the time, my dad was dismayed that I would prioritize personality over policy. His reaction didn't resonate with me then, but over the years, I have realized that while I admired the candidate as an individual, I disagreed with many of his policies. Some of his positions conflicted with my convictions, though he was born-again. I'm not saying he was wrong on all fronts, but he took stances that opposed beliefs I held dear—beliefs that the other candidate, in contrast, supported. I then understood why my dad was so bewildered by my decision. I bring this up because it highlights the importance of evaluating candidates based on both their integrity and the policies they promote. Ultimately, our votes should reflect not just admiration (or dislike) for a person but a thoughtful alignment with the principles and values we hold dear.

You must vote based on your most heart-felt convictions—what I have developed as the ABCs of Politics. Surprisingly, I have heard that less than 10% of our population consider these factors before voting:

Abortion – Addressing the moral, legal, and societal implications of abortion rights and restrictions.

Borders – Discussing the importance of national borders, immigration policies, and border security.

Constitutional Beliefs – Covering debates on traditional interpretations, constitutional reconstruction, and their influence on governance.

Debt – Covering national and personal debt issues, fiscal policies, and economic strategies to manage debt.

Environmentalism – Focusing on climate change, conservation, pollution control, sustainable energy initiatives, and energy independence.

Freedom of Speech – Emphasizing the right to express opinions freely and the implications of censorship.

Gun Rights – Discussing the Second Amendment, gun control measures, and the debate over firearm regulations.

Healthcare – Exploring the debate over public vs. private healthcare systems, insurance, and access to medical care.

Identity Politics – Examining race, gender, sexual orientation, LGBTQ+ rights, and their role in shaping policies and societal divisions.

Justice System – Addressing criminal justice reform, prison system issues, law enforcement practices, and public safety concerns.

K-12 Education – Discussing primary and secondary education challenges, school funding, and curriculum standards.

Labor Laws – Covering workers' rights, minimum wage debates, employment regulations, and corporate governance.

Military – Focusing on defense policies, veterans' issues, and the military budget.

National Security – Discussing terrorism, cybersecurity, foreign policy, and border protection strategies.

Opioid Crisis – Addressing the public health emergency related to opioid addiction and possible solutions.

Privacy – Focusing on data protection, government surveillance, and individual privacy rights.

Quality of Life – Considering issues like poverty, housing, infra-structure, economic inequality, and public services affecting daily living standards.

Religious Freedom – Emphasizing the right to practice and express one's faith without government interference.

Social Security – Discussing the future of social security programs and the sustainability of these safety nets.

Taxation – Covering tax policy debates, rates, corporate regulations, and economic impacts on different income groups.

Unemployment – Addressing joblessness, job training, and employment assistance programs.

Welfare – Discussing social assistance programs, universal basic income, eligibility debates, and reparations.

Voting Rights – Addressing voter suppression, election integrity, money in politics, and the influence of lobbyists.

Xenophobia – Focusing on combating prejudice, promoting diversity, and the challenges related to DEI (Diversity, Equity, and Inclusion).

Youth Programs – Highlighting education, job training, and support initiatives for young people.

Zero Tolerance Policies – Covering strict enforcement policies in areas like crime, drug use, and immigration.

As a Christ follower, I want to challenge you to examine these ABCs and decide what you believe and why. Do you believe your voting style aligns with the convictions and truths in the Bible? Are you engaging in society in a way that supports the policies you want to see the government implement?

I surface this information since it is vital for every Christ-follower to be thoughtful and prayerful about such matters. But I also created this framework to ask how we speak and act toward unbelievers and believers when sharing our convictions and promoting the candidate of our choice. Does how we speak and act draw others to see the good behind our convictions and beliefs?

Let me reiterate: when we must take a stand, we must take a stand. Even Peter took a stand in the Book of Acts. His words in Acts 5:29, "We must obey God rather than men," remind us that our ultimate loyalty is to God, not societal norms. However, Peter also teaches that standing firm doesn't mean abandoning good behavior. We must speak truth boldly but always with humility, grace, and love. In today's polarized climate, Peter's guidance is more relevant than ever: let your good deeds speak for you.

When we maintain "excellent behavior" and keep a "good conscience," we ensure that our position, though clearly in opposition to another group, person, or policy, is beyond reproach.

Taking a stand in this manner means engaging our beliefs with grace, truth, and love rather than with hatred and disdain. By doing so, even those who oppose or slander us may eventually recognize the goodness of our convictions and compassion. Our consistent, honorable conduct can lead them to realize that their criticisms are unfounded. This approach requires courage to stand firm and wisdom to do so in a way that exemplifies the heart of Christ.

We must ensure that if they object to anything, it is our policy beliefs, not our bad personality!

I understand—it's easy to feel compelled to express frustration because it seems like we're living in the worst of times. But this sense of urgency isn't unique to our generation. If we look at history, such as the Civil War in the 1800s, where brothers fought against each other, even to the death, over the issue of slavery, this puts things into perspective. As troubling as today's political climate may be, we must not lose hope or believe there's no way forward. Let me add, which is an undercurrent belief I hold as I write this book, that during the American Civil War, widespread religious revivals, known as "army revivals," swept through both the Union and Confederate armies. Estimates suggest that between 100,000 to 200,000 Union soldiers and at least 100,000 Confederate soldiers came to Christ. These revivals crossed denominational lines, taking place across various battlefronts and involving soldiers from all social classes. As we live above the bar, let's pray to this end.[1]

We all know non-Christians who hold themselves to Christ-like standards—such as emotional intelligence, integrity, and compassion. Being made in the image of God, they naturally aspire to be the best versions of themselves, often finding research to support the very values we see in Scripture. When we embody these qualities while speaking truth to power, we align with what the world instinctively knows is the right way to live. However, when we fall short in the twelve areas discussed, we give the world a reason to dismiss the message of Christ altogether.

Let us not be the cause of their disbelief.

As the Bible says, even when slandered, "they will have nothing bad to say about us" because we live above the bar. By doing so, we, as Christians, can authentically engage with a world that is watching, bringing conviction and compassion into the light.

But, beyond politics, a more significant thrust of this book is that when we live above the bar, we will find someone knocking on our door at 3 a.m. in crisis saying, "I am at the end of my rope, and I need help. I have watched you, and I want what you have." May we be the kind of neighbors and Christians whose homes they feel comfortable coming to, even at 3 a.m., when they need someone the most and open their hearts to Christ Himself.

Emerson Eggerichs, Ph.D.
United States Election Season, Fall 2024

Introduction

The world has long applauded certain traits—resilience, adaptability, emotional intelligence, and integrity. Research in psychology, business, and social sciences consistently shows that people who embody these qualities thrive personally and professionally. Books, seminars, and educational programs teach these virtues, and the secular world recognizes and respects those who master them. We often hear the world invite their particular audience to be the best version of themselves. For example, the best version might be the person who "keeps their cool," "thinks outside the box," and when not first succeeding, "bounces back stronger." There is admiration for the person who manages time effectively, learns continuously, and approaches life with discipline.

Christians are called to live according to biblical wisdom, which often aligns with the world's understanding of these traits.

Proverbs 24:16 says, "For though the righteous fall seven times, they rise again," illustrating the importance of resilience in the Christian life.

However, what happens when believers fail to embody these characteristics, particularly in ways that the world values?

When Christians crumble under adversity or disagreement, react poorly to challenges, or fail to manage their resources and time well, it raises a critical question: What does this reflect of our faith in Christ? Suppose unbelievers, who may not know the deeper spiritual truths of the Bible, can demonstrate resilience, creativity, and integrity. Why do some believers struggle to show these same virtues, especially when Scripture calls us to embody them? Someone gave me a great insight on why we might not live above the bar: "This makes me question the WHY behind it all—why some Christians don't act in a moral or respectable way. It seems that some Christians may believe they are simply 'covered' by their acceptance of Christ and grace, and therefore, their actions don't need to justify their faith. Growing up, I often heard that we are saved by grace, not acts. It raises the question: Do some Christians feel safe because of 'grace' and 'faith' alone, without considering the importance of their actions and moral standards?"

Years ago, a well-known pastor said he visited a jail to meet with prisoners. One of the prisoners recognized the pastor and verbally praised this pastor's teachings, telling the pastor he had

In this book, I will share stories of people I've met through pastoring and counseling and the tens of thousands of testimonies I've received through email. These are people who were doing their best to live above the bar.

listened to most of his sermons. The pastor asked why he was in jail, and the man said, "Oh, there are about a hundred parking tickets I have refused to pay, and I won't pay them. The authorities are so stupid." This pastor looked at the man and said, "Can I ask you to do me a favor?" The man excitedly answered, "Yes, anything. What?" The pastor said, "Don't tell anybody that you are a Christian. You will discredit the faith."

The gap between what the world (and the Bible) expects and what some Christians practice can damage our witness. How many unbelievers remain unconvinced about the relevance of Christianity because the believers in their lives live below the bar set even by secular standards? This is not just a question of moral failure but of neglecting fundamental life skills that God calls us to develop and apply.

In this book, I will share stories of people I've met through pastoring and counseling and the tens of thousands of testimonies I've received through email. These are people who were doing their best to live above the bar.

ONE

Emotional Intelligence
(Keep Your Cool)

When was the last time you "lost your cool?" We've all been there, even though Christians should, in theory, lead the world in emotional intelligence. Yet, we don't always practice what we preach. Ironically, as we will discuss throughout this book, many who don't profess to follow Christ often live out His teachings on emotional intelligence better than we do! A quick walk down the self-help aisle at Barnes and Noble reveals a widespread desire to excel in self-regulation and emotional growth. Traits like controlling anger, managing stress with self-awareness, and practicing empathy are highly valued and pursued. We strengthen relationships, promote peace, and gain greater self-awareness by actively working on our emotional intelligence. And here's the best part: Scripture fully supports this!

Let's consider anger as an example. Someone prone to outbursts (Galatians 5:20) is not advancing God's purposes in the world. Scripture is clear: "Everyone must be quick to hear, slow to speak, and slow to anger; for a man's anger does not bring about the righteousness of God" (James 1:19-20).

In my correspondence, some people have reflected on their past behavior and shared their experiences like this:

"I used to explode over the smallest frustrations. My anger drove a wedge between my extended family and me. But when I truly embraced James 1:19, God began to heal my relationships and replace my rage with peace. I realized family members weren't rejecting the things I believed but were offended by me."

"I felt justified in my anger at work, thinking I was defending my integrity. But the more I lashed out, the more isolated I became. It wasn't until I surrendered my temper to God and embraced James' command to be slow to anger that I saw a true change in my relationships and my witness."

"For years, my anger defined me. I thought it made me strong, but it was a mask for my insecurity and inadequacies."

"I was known for my temper, even in my church. It was my 'thorn in the flesh.' But God showed me that I couldn't be a vessel of His love while harboring so much anger."

"I justified my anger as 'righteous indignation,' but God's Word exposed the truth: my anger wasn't serving His purposes. It was serving my pride."

The world respects those who manage their emotions. Suppose we wish to be skilled communicators, which we will consider in another chapter and address at length in my book *Speak Your Mind: Evaluating and Unleashing Your Communication Strengths.* In that case, we must begin with internal, mature self-regulation. Then, we can demonstrate the effects of our self-regulation through strengthened communication skills. Research on emotional intelligence consistently shows that controlling anger leads to healthier relationships and better outcomes. While the secular world might not always be perfect in self-regulation, it still expects how they and even Christians should behave. When a Christian loses their temper, it leaves a lasting negative impression on unbelievers, damaging their view of that Christian's faith. It isn't rocket science that we ought to live up to our proclaimed values and beliefs. When we fail to exhibit emotional self-regulation, we feed the skeptics' skepticism.

I've seen pastors, missionaries, and theologians—despite their ministries—lose favor with their children due to uncontrolled anger. Their failure to manage their temper within the family led some of their children to walk away from the faith or never come to Christ at all. It's sobering to think how damaging a lack of emotional control can be for one's witness and closest relationships. A lack of emotional self-regulation makes those on the receiving end feel unheard, unseen, and, in some cases, unsafe. A lack of self-control can cause severe damage and break trust.

The world sees emotional intelligence as a strength. In chaos, emotional intelligence can bring peace and wisdom and deepen trust. Managed emotions keep fuel from being added to a fire and can put the fire completely out. When believers fail to model this, it undermines the testimony of Christ. We are not cool when we lose our cool. While a believer may speak of Jesus, their actions and attitudes ultimately shape how others perceive their faith. Christians must strive to exemplify self-control, especially in challenging situations, as a reflection of God's work in their lives.

I love what this person said: "When provoked, I seek to remain emotionally self-controlled and avoid brash, unwise responses."

Many people have often come to Christ by being witnessed to simply through observing positive changes in someone they knew. The witness of Christ in a softened life is powerful. The unbeliever asks, "Who are you, and what happened to you?"

I became a Christian at 16 after attending a Billy Graham film called *For Pete's Sake*. After that, my mother came to Christ. Shortly after that, my sister Ann came to faith because of what she had observed in my mom. Though my dad struggled with rage and shame, he eventually came to Christ, too. The effects in his life were so transformative that he wanted his nearest and dearest to know the love of Christ, too. Since I was the "family pastor," so to speak, my dad asked me to meet with his best friend, Charlie Ellis, and his brother, Andy Eggerichs. I led both to Christ because they had seen the change in my dad and were curious to know more. My dad's new approach to life created a bridge that enabled me to walk across it to talk to Charlie and my uncle.

The importance of emotional control is not just for personal peace but for the witness of Christ to a watching world. People like my dad, myself, and any human who acknowledges their failure and need for Christ's forgiveness can believe that they are not too far gone, that it is a new day, and to move forward differently. This difference will create a curiosity in others.

A pastor friend with a street ministry in a significant city confessed that he lost his temper at a meat market one day. Having grown up as the town rowdy and street fighter, Christ changed him, but not 100%. A fellow had cut in front of him and cursed him, so my friend took a pound of freshly ground hamburger and shoved it in his face. We could objectively say, "The guy who cut and cursed for no reason was a jerk." Immediately, my friend humbled himself and sought the man's forgiveness, confessing that his actions were wrong. This action stunned the man, who became meek and apologized for the cut. In this, my pastor friend recognized the bigger picture here. He had a reputation in that metropolitan area for Christ and the Kingdom. Defaulting to his street fighting days would never bring that man at the counter to Christ.

We cannot tell people to "go to hell" and then tell them of Jesus so they won't.

As followers of Christ, we are called to engage with patience and grace, leaving the ultimate outcomes in God's hands. When we resort to anger, we risk becoming like the people whose behavior we critique or claim to be freed from in Christ. This doesn't mean we remain passive in the face of injustice or compromise our convictions, but it does mean that we trust the power of truth, prayer, and civil discourse to bring about real change.

Our approach at work, online, over politics, with neighbors, and even with other Christians should reflect our confidence in God's sovereignty over all situations. We have a greater calling to live in a way that reflects Christ, especially when the temptation to fight back is strong. Through patience, civility, and faith, we reveal a power far greater than anything the world can muster.

Even when the people in our lives ignore the substance of our ideas, don't empathize with our point of view, attack our character, or misunderstand our motives, we must not justify a less-than-Christ-like response. We must live above the bar and not grow weary. In time, we will find that keeping our cool will open more doors, heal relationships, and support our testimony to others.

What the Scripture Says on Emotional Control

The Bible has much to say about controlling our emotions, particularly anger. Proverbs 16:32 states, "Better a patient person than a warrior, one with self-control than one who takes a city." This highlights that patience and emotional restraint are more valuable than physical strength. Ecclesiastes 7:9 reminds us, "Do not be quickly provoked in your spirit, for anger resides in the lap of fools." These scriptures reflect the spiritual importance of controlling our emotions, which goes beyond mere relational success—it reflects godliness.

Jesus Himself modeled emotional control, even under extreme pressure. When mocked, insulted, and beaten, He did not retaliate angrily but remained composed, demonstrating ultimate emotional intelligence by trusting His Father's plan (1 Peter 2:23).

Yes, Jesus felt and evidenced anger, but it was controlled and rooted in holy indignation. Mark tells us in Mark 3:5 (NIV): "He looked around at them in anger and, deeply distressed at their stubborn hearts, said to the man, 'Stretch out your hand.' He stretched it out, and his hand was completely restored." And most of us know what He did in the Temple area. We read in John 2:16, "So he made a whip out of cords, and drove all from the temple courts, sheep and cattle; he scattered the money changers' coins and overturned their tables. He said to those who sold doves, 'Get these out of here! Stop turning my Father's house into a market!'" In these unique historical moments, his anger was never rooted in personal retaliation or uncontrolled rage. Because Jesus demonstrated emotional regulation, his moments of anger greatly impacted those around him. His anger was justified and heard. Certainly, anyone who uses the example of Jesus should first turn the other cheek and pray for their enemies, especially as Jesus did,

"Father, forgive them; they know not what they do." First things first. Furthermore, Jesus was not violent toward people and told Peter, "Put your sword back in its place, for all who draw the sword will die by the sword" (Matthew 26:52).

Could This Be You?

Below are some composite testimonies I have personally received or heard from people in conversations. They worked on what triggered their anger and soon discovered the benefits of "keeping their cool."

"In an online debate, I could feel the insults flying, but I decided not to engage in the negativity. I responded calmly, focusing on the issue rather than the personal attacks. One person messaged me privately, saying they respected my approach and wanted to learn more about my views."

"While discussing gun control with a friend, I kept my emotions in check even though I strongly disagreed. This made the conversation more constructive, and we could exchange ideas without getting angry."

"My husband and I are healing rage-aholics, and my children are a product of this battleground. I went ballistic over the state of my son's car. My husband quietly asked me to stop. I mocked him but continued my tirade. I later felt shame and said, 'Lord, I am unrighteous and unholy, and

"In an online debate, I could feel the insults flying, but I decided not to engage in the negativity. I responded calmly, focusing on the issue rather than the personal attacks. One person messaged me privately, saying they respected my approach and wanted to learn more about my views."

I don't want to act like this anymore.' [It was then] God gave me strength and peace...God showed me hope in the face of adversity."

"I was on a debate panel for a local political event, and my opponent started getting personal. Instead of retaliating, I remained calm and focused on the issues. Afterward, people approached me to say they appreciated how I handled myself and the debate."

Practical Applications for Emotional Intelligence

For Christians, managing our emotions, especially anger, is not optional—it's a biblical mandate. But how can we practically apply this in our daily lives? Here are a few strategies:

Prayer for Patience: Pray for the Holy Spirit to give you patience and emotional control. Ask God to help you grow in these areas (Galatians 5:22-23). Over the years of pastoral ministry, I have heard this kind of testimony. "I struggled for years with impatience and frustration, often taking it out on those closest to me. It hurt my relationships and left me feeling like a failure. One day, I read Galatians 5:22-23, and it was like God was speaking directly to me. I began praying daily, asking the Holy Spirit to fill me with patience and self-control. It wasn't an instant change, but little by little, I felt a calmness growing within me. I started responding to situations with patience, not from me but from God. When

I feel the old anger rising, I stop and pray, trusting the Spirit to help me grow in grace and love."

Reflection on Scripture: Meditate on scriptures encouraging emotional restraint, like James 1:19-20 and Proverbs 14:29 ("Whoever is patient has great understanding, but one who is quick-tempered displays folly"). Let these verses remind you of the power and necessity of controlling your temper, as it did with this person. "I'll never forget the day I almost lost a dear friend because of my uncontrolled temper. I felt so justified in my anger, but later, I stumbled upon Proverbs 14:29: 'Whoever is patient has great understanding, but one who is quick-tempered displays folly.' The truth in that verse hit me hard. I saw myself as a fool, letting my temper ruin relationships. As odd as it sounds, that day, I said to myself, 'It's time to stop being an idiot.' Now, whenever I feel my temper flaring, I recite that verse to myself, 'This person isn't causing me to be angry—they are revealing my choice to be angry.' I may be right, but I don't have to be an angry fool to prove it."

Accountability Partners: Find someone who can hold you accountable when you struggle with emotional control. Confession and accountability can be powerful tools for healing and growth (James 5:16). "I used to deny that I had an anger problem, but I was wrong. My anger kept hurting the people I loved, especially my wife. Eventually, I had to face the truth and swallow my pride. I asked my best friend to be my accountability partner. I confessed my struggles to him, and instead of judging me, he prayed with me. Whenever I felt my temper rising, I would text him, and his words of encouragement would calm me down. It has been life-changing to have someone who truly understands my struggle and is willing to walk with me through it."

Take a Pause: When anger rises, pause and breathe before responding. Reflecting before reacting can prevent an emotional outburst (Proverbs 15:1, "A gentle answer turns away wrath, but a harsh word stirs up anger"). It does work as reflected in this person's journey. "I used to think that pausing and taking a deep breath was just a cliché, something people said but didn't mean. It felt superficial like it couldn't help with the fire that raged inside me. But one day, after a heated argument with my adult son, I decided to try it. I took a deep breath and walked away momentarily instead of shouting back. As I calmed down, I remembered Proverbs 15:1: 'A gentle answer turns away wrath, but a harsh word stirs up anger.' It struck me that this is what it means to be slow to anger. When I returned, I spoke calmly, and instead of escalating, we had a meaningful conversation. I realized then that pausing isn't a weakness—it's a strength. It's choosing peace over conflict."

Focus on Humility: Often, our anger stems from pride or feeling disrespected. Practicing humility can reduce the likelihood of losing control (Philippians 2:3-4). Remember, Jesus was humble, even when He had every reason to respond otherwise. I rejoice when I hear testimonies along this line. "For years, I struggled with anger, especially when I felt disrespected. I saw every slight as a challenge to my authority and worth. I didn't realize my anger was just a reaction to my insecurity and pride. But then I read about Jesus' humility in Philippians 2:3-4 and realized that true strength lies in humility, not in proving myself. I started reflecting on this during moments of conflict, which softened how I reacted. I also learned about emotional intelligence, especially keeping my cool, and that became a new goal in my life since I value intelligence. I began focusing on listening rather than defending, valuing others' perspectives above my own. My emotional intelligence grew, and I found that people responded to me with more respect and understanding."

Emotional Intelligence as a Christian Responsibility

While the secular world values emotional intelligence for professional success and healthy relationships, Christians are called to practice it as a reflection of Christ. The world's motivation might be self-improvement, but it is about godliness for Christians. Self-control is not just a skill; it's part of the fruit of the Spirit (Galatians 5:22-23). When we practice emotional control, we reflect the work of the Holy Spirit in our lives. Our emotional intelligence becomes a testimony to our belief in the presence of Christ, who indwells us.

As Christians, our emotional control should not just meet the world's expectations but exceed them.

So, how do your actions reflect Christ when you're under pressure? When provoked or frustrated, do you respond gracefully or let your emotions take control? Reflect on your behavior and how it aligns with the self-control Christ calls us to embody. The next time you're tempted to lose your temper or not be considerate of "the other," consider how your response might affect your witness to those around you. Your actions speak louder than your words, and emotional intelligence, especially in difficult situations, can be the very thing that draws someone to ask, "What's different about you?"

None of us are perfect; we all fall short, but God's grace is sufficient. If you've struggled with emotional control or awareness, there is hope for change through Christ. The journey to emotional maturity is part of growing in sanctification. As you seek to honor God in this area, remember Philippians 4:13, "I can do all this through him who gives me strength."

Let this be an encouragement that, with God's help, you can grow in emotional intelligence and become a living testimony to those around you.

TWO

Resilience
(Bounce Back Stronger)

Resilience means that when times get tough, the tough keeps going. We reject the idea that if you don't succeed at first, quit. Instead, we bounce back stronger. Showing perseverance for the sake of the vision or task and God's purpose in our lives compels us to keep running the race. Resilience is a vital quality that empowers us to overcome setbacks, stay committed to our goals, and ultimately fulfill God's purposes. It means being able to bounce back from failure, learn from mistakes, and keep pressing forward despite obstacles. Resilience allows us to stay the course, even silently, believing there will be sowing.

I was once told a story of a grandmother who persistently prayed for her grandson, even though he didn't come to faith until years later. Despite his indifference and even hostility towards religion, her unwavering prayers and faith were eventually answered when he turned to Christ. This story highlights the impact of resilience in prayer and faith and demonstrates how steadfast intercession can lead to glorious outcomes. Many of us would share that we do not give up in prayer in hearing such stories. My wife Sarah testifies to the impact of such people who kept interceding when not succeeding in prayer at first.

When we persevere with integrity, we offer a living example of what it means to trust God in the ups and downs of life, making our lives a witness to His sustaining grace. Our ability to endure and remain steadfast can plant seeds of faith, reflecting our hope and strength in Christ.

What the Scripture Says on Resilience

- **Proverbs 24:16**: "For a righteous person falls seven times and rises again."
- **Proverbs 14:23**: "All hard work brings a profit, but mere talk leads only to poverty."
- **Ecclesiastes 9:10**: "Whatever your hand finds to do, do it with all your might..."
- **Ecclesiastes 11:6**: "Sow your seed in the morning, and at evening let your hands not be idle, for you do not know which will succeed, whether this or that, or whether both will do equally well."

- **Galatians 6:9:** "Let us not become weary in doing good, for at the proper time we will reap a harvest if we do not give up."

- **Joshua 1:8:** "This book of the law shall not depart from your mouth, but you shall meditate on it day and night, so that you may be careful to do according to all that is written in it; for then you will make your way prosperous, and then you will have success."

The Bible repeatedly highlights the importance of diligence and perseverance and encourages us to stick with it. Knocked down? Get back up. Be diligent, persistent, and faithful in our efforts. Trust that God will bring fruit from our labor in His perfect timing. Follow Him, and there will be fruit for the Kingdom and, often, success in a worldly sense.

However, biblical wisdom goes beyond just working hard—it also encourages working smart. As shared above, Ecclesiastes 11:6 reflects the idea of sowing seeds in the morning and evening, increasing the chances of success. This principle speaks to the importance of trying multiple approaches and not giving up after one attempt. Our resilience and adaptability, especially when aligned with God's guidance, can lead to remarkable outcomes.

Discover Your Life Message Through Your Resilience During Setbacks

Resilience gives us the strength to see things through, reaping rewards we may not have seen if we had given up. Resilience can completely transform our lives and be a testament to others who witness transformations that come from seeing something through. Take a look at these testimonies people have shared with me to understand the power of resilience:

Rebuilding a Career: After being laid off from his job, a man was devastated but decided to pursue a new field he was passionate about. Despite initial failures and rejections, he kept applying and studying. He kept entrusting himself to God. After three years, he finally secured a position that exceeded his previous job, both in satisfaction and salary. His persistence paid off, and he now encourages others never to give up on their dreams. They listen to him because he has been where they find themselves.

Saving a Marriage: A couple faced severe marital problems, including financial strain and communication breakdowns. Instead of giving up, they decided to seek godly, wise counseling. It took years of hard work, but today, they share their story to help others facing similar challenges, proving that resilience can save even the most troubled marriages.

Overcoming Addiction: After struggling with substance abuse for over a decade, a man finally sought help. He relapsed several times, but each time, he got back up and continued his recovery journey. He has now been sober for seven years and works as a counselor to help others find hope and resilience in their battles. Do you think others seek his wisdom and even learn from his determination after setbacks? Yes.

Starting a Business After Bankruptcy: A woman's first business venture ended in bankruptcy. It was a crushing blow, but she learned from her mistakes and launched a new business. This time, she succeeded and turned it into a thriving enterprise. Her story is a testament to the power of resilience and learning from past failures.

Ministry Perseverance: A pastor faced criticism and declining attendance in his church. Instead of resigning, he prayed, sought mentorship, and made gradual changes. It took years, but the congregation grew, and the church became a beacon of hope in the community. His commitment to God's call, despite opposition, inspired many.

Writing Success After Rejection: An author faced rejection after rejection from publishers. She could have given up, but instead, she independently published her book. It gained popularity and was eventually picked up by a major publisher, becoming a bestseller. Her story encourages aspiring writers not to give up on their craft.

Finding Faith After Tragedy: A woman lost her child in a tragic accident and felt utterly broken. Over time, she found strength in her faith and began to speak to others about grief and healing. Her resilience in the face of unimaginable loss has brought comfort and hope to countless others.

Sports Comeback: After a severe injury, an athlete was told he would never play professionally again. He underwent rigorous rehabilitation and worked tirelessly to return to his sport. Against all odds, he fully recovered and had a successful career. His story is a powerful example of physical and mental resilience.

Recovery from a Public Failure: A public figure faced humiliation after a major career mistake. Rather than retreating from the public eye, he owned up to his error, made amends, and worked tirelessly to rebuild his reputation. His honesty and resilience turned a failure into a story of redemption and integrity.

These examples demonstrate that perseverance is key to success in various aspects of life and should also be a value for Christians. The secular world applauds resilience when faced with failure. Everyone could recount a powerful "come back" story that touched them. Few differ from the commonly quoted axiom, "If at first you don't succeed, try again." As Christians, we are called to model resilience, as it demonstrates how God is constantly at work, making all things new.

A Challenge to the Reader

Do you approach challenges resiliently, bounce back stronger, or give up after the first failure? Are you easily defeated when something doesn't work out or if you entirely fall short? Whether in your personal life, marriage, or ministry, ask yourself: Am I willing to try again when things don't go as planned?

As Christians, we are called to persevere. Dr. Raymon Edman, former President of Wheaton College, espoused a simple truth: "It is too soon to quit." Winston Churchill famously said, "Never give in. Never give in. Never, never, never, never—in nothing, great or small, large or petty—never give in, except to convictions of honor and good sense."

If you've been struggling in your marriage, your work, or your ministry, keep at it. If we are doing the good and right things, don't stop. My friend, Don Cousins, always counseled his son Kirk Cousins, an NFL quarterback, with simple advice: "Make good decisions, and good things happen. Make bad decisions, and bad things happen."

A Little of My Story

My life has had moments of defeat, and I learned about resilience. As a young boy, I faced significant challenges in school. When my parents separated for five years, the turmoil at home deeply impacted me. I began third grade with a report card full of Ds, reflecting my troubled mind. However, my teacher, Mrs. Smith, saw potential in me that I couldn't see in myself. She constantly encouraged me, saying, "You can do it," even when I doubted. Through her unwavering support and my determination, I turned things around by the end of the year, earning all As. Her words at the end of third grade still echo in my ears 65 years later: "See, I told you that you could do it!" That experience taught me the power of resilience and perseverance, showing me that success is possible if we press on despite personal struggles.

During my time at military school, from 8th to 12th grade, I wasn't the most talented student, but I stayed year after year, setting goals and working diligently. My perseverance paid off when, in my senior year, my classmates voted me "most likely to succeed." The older I get, the more meaningful that recognition becomes to me, as it serves as a powerful reminder that success often comes not from being the smartest but from remaining faithful and persistent.

As a side note, over twenty years later, a former cadet visited the church I pastored. He came to share my impact on his life during our time at the academy, though I had no idea then. Despite us not being in touch all those years, his visit revealed a spiritual hunger planted long ago. I had the privilege of leading him to Christ during his visit, a powerful reminder that the seeds we plant through consistent faith (I came to Christ my sophomore year and sought to identify with Him until I graduated) and resilience can bear fruit, even after many years.

In the early years of my ministry, Sarah and I faced numerous challenges as we worked to build and lead a congregation. I remember reassuring her when she wondered if we could do it all. "Honey, we're in this for the long haul. We'll just plod along,

In the early years of my
ministry, Sarah and I faced
numerous challenges as
we worked to build and
lead a congregation. I
remember reassuring
her when she wondered
if we could do it all.
"Honey, we're in this
for the long haul. We'll
just plod along, loving
people and serving faithfully."

loving people and serving faithfully." That relieved her. It made perfect sense. We will plod. That commitment to perseverance became our guiding principle. Despite conflicts, personal struggles, and the daily challenges of ministry, we remained steadfast. This mindset has sustained us over the years and has become a testament to others about staying the course. We have seen how resilience, rooted in love and dedication, can transform lives and communities, reflecting the enduring love of Christ.

These experiences have shown me that our resilience and refusal to quit, even in the face of challenges, can be a powerful testimony to others. It's not just about personal success; it's about living out our faith consistently, no matter the obstacles. When people see us sticking with our tasks, remaining faithful to our commitments, and ultimately finding success, they notice something different. They begin to see that our perseverance is not driven by sheer willpower alone but by a deeper trust in God's purposes for our lives.

Seven Big Questions to Ask Yourself

1. Pursuit of Goals: *When faced with setbacks in pursuing my goals, do I adjust my strategy and keep moving forward, or do I allow discouragement to stop me?*

2. Physical and Mental Well-being: *Am I consistent in taking care of my physical and mental health, even when progress seems slow or I experience setbacks?*

3. Career and Professional Growth: *Do I proactively seek opportunities for growth and development in my career, and how do I handle rejection or professional setbacks?*

4. Relationships and Community: *Am I committed to investing in my relationships, even when conflicts or misunderstandings arise, or do I withdraw?*

5. Creative and Intellectual Pursuits: *Do I continue to explore and express my creative or intellectual interests despite criticism or initial failure?*

6. Personal Growth and Character Development: *How do I respond to challenges in developing my character, such as practicing patience or integrity, when I fall short of my own expectations?*

7. Adaptability and Learning: *Am I willing to adapt and learn from new experiences, or do I resist change and avoid feedback that could help me grow?*

Practical Applications for Resilience

Take Care of Your Body: Mental clarity is essential for resilience. To keep your mind sharp, ensure you're fueling your body well, getting adequate sleep, and exercising often. (More on this in the Growth in Wellness section.) This will improve your overall outlook and give you the energy to bounce back!

Practice with Something Small: Think of something you've "failed" at recently or even something that didn't go how you thought or hoped it would. Maybe you didn't get the promotion you wanted, or you got a flat tire on your way to an important event, which made you late. What was your initial reaction to the disappointment, and how can you change your view of it with a resilient mindset?

Keep Things in Perspective: This life will have disappointments, and many of them. Remember the testimonies in the chapter and keep perspective when something knocks you down. We all face troubles. How can you bounce back?

Overcoming Hurdles and Finding Faith

I need to insert here that I do not make light of evil. Evil can defeat us. Satan would not keep scheming against us if he failed each time. How do we try again when what we have experienced is pure evil? This isn't about failing to succeed and trying again; this is about surviving unimaginable trauma and finding the courage to hope again.

One individual shared with me the unimaginable hardships she had faced in life: a father who killed his girlfriend and himself, a mother who attempted suicide, and a foster parent who molested her. Later, she experienced manipulation from her husband. Initially, she prayed for a change in her circumstances, but when her prayers seemed unanswered, she turned away from God. Yet, through this painful journey, she discovered that God worked in ways she couldn't see. Her return to faith became a powerful testimony of enduring dark times and trusting in God's plan, even when it's not visible.

Grace and Encouragement

Remember, God is with us in every challenge we face. Sometimes, the solution doesn't come right away, and that's okay. The important thing is to keep trying, persevere, and trust that God is working through our efforts. Galatians 6:9 reminds us, "Let us not become weary in doing good, for at the proper time we will reap a harvest if we do not give up."

Take heart if you've been discouraged because things haven't worked out as expected. God's grace is sufficient, and with His help, you can find the solutions you need. Keep sowing, working, and trusting that the harvest will come in time.

THREE

Stewardship in Finances
(A Penny Saved Is a Penny Earned)

Good stewardship of finances honors God, enables us to serve His purposes, and serves our families by keeping us free from the bondage of debt. When we manage money wisely, we reflect Christ's lordship in our lives, setting an example for others. However, financial mismanagement can hinder our witness; non-Christians may question our ability to counsel them on spiritual matters if we cannot demonstrate responsible decision-making in our own lives. Effective financial management, therefore, is not just about providing for our families, but also about showcasing the peace and freedom found in Christ to a watching world.

Let me say that we must work hard to earn money to save money and spend money on what we need. But it's essential to add that we must also earn money to share with others. Perhaps giving is where we need to start.

The Importance of Giving

Arthur C. Brooks, a professor at Harvard, wrote an article, "Why Giving Matters." His findings blew his mind. He knew that prosperous people gave more money. It was a simple math equation. But what he did not believe is that those who give become more prosperous:

> "Specifically, here's what I found: Say you have two identical families—same religion, same race, same number of kids, same town, same level of education—everything's the same, except that one family gives $100 more to charity than the second family. Then the giving family will earn on average $375 more in income than the non-giving family—and that's statistically attributable to the gift."

In discovering this, he wrote, "The more I ran the numbers, the more I kept getting this crazy result. But still, I refused to believe it. In desperation, I finally went to a colleague who specialized in the psychology of charitable giving. 'I'm getting this result I can't understand,' I told him. 'It doesn't make sense. It's like the hand of God or something on the economy, and I can't believe it's true.'"

"Why don't you believe it's true?" he asked me. "You're a Christian, aren't you?"

This shook me a bit, but just for a second. "Yeah, but I'm also a social scientist," I shot back. "We're not supposed to believe those things."[2]

But the truth was inescapable based on the data. Even so, I love Brooks's article,

"John D. Rockefeller believed that he was rich because he gave so much, and throughout his life, before he was a rich man, he gave a lot. He was a charitable person. A lot of entrepreneurs believe that one of the reasons that they're rich is because they give. Entrepreneurs in this country are some of its most charitable citizens. I've always heard this because, for years, I taught in a department of entrepreneurship, so I got to know the modern John D. Rockefellers who thought that they were rich partly because they gave. But, you know, I never believed it—never believed a word of it—because I was trained as an economist."

Brooks now believes.

But most of us believed this first because Jesus said in Luke 6:38, "Give, and it will be given to you. A good measure, pressed down, shaken together, and running over, will be poured into your lap. For with the measure you use, it will be measured to you."

I surface the concept of generosity since I have a hunch that those who first commit to the tithe, which most apply to be 10%, get their financial household in order first and foremost to follow this instruction. And, they do so with a measure of excitement. Two Scriptures meant a great deal to Sarah and me when we first married. We acted on these and have never looked back:

- **Malachi 3:10 (NIV):** "Bring the whole tithe into the storehouse, that there may be food in my house. Test me in this," says the Lord Almighty, "and see if I will not throw open the floodgates of heaven and pour out so much blessing that there will not be room enough to store it."

- **Proverbs 3:9-10 (NIV):** "Honor the Lord with your wealth, with the first fruits of all your crops; then your barns will be filled to overflowing, and your vats will brim over with new wine."

The challenge I wish to extend is simple, but it sounds odd to most: make your primary goal to give (i.e., 10%) and work back from there. Ask God to enable you to work, work hard, save, and have enough to spend on what is needed. In the long haul, the Lord gives us more than we need. As Paul wrote, He "who richly provides us with everything for our enjoyment" (1 Timothy 6:17, 18).

The secret to wise stewardship is first generosity, giving off the top and to the cause of Christ. Apart from God blessing the givers, such givers must put their financial house in order and do nothing to prevent honoring the Lord first. Let me add: there is only one place in the Scripture where God calls the believer to test Him. We all know that we are not to test the Lord in a bad way, but when it comes to the tithe that we bring to Him, He calls us to test Him—test Him to see what He will do in response.

Therefore, it requires us to be good stewards who work hard. This means living within our means, saving diligently, giving generously, and buying and investing wisely to honor God. It also involves being content with what we have and avoiding greed and overindulgence. Following these principles reflects God's wisdom and faithfulness in managing the blessings He has entrusted us.

The secular world has long understood the importance of financial prudence. The phrase "a penny saved is a penny earned" captures a core principle of living within one's means, saving for the future, and ensuring long-term financial stability. The world respects this, and research from Harvard found it to be an incredibly happy way to live.

What the Scripture Says on Financial Responsibility

- **Proverbs 21:5 (NIV):** "The plans of the diligent lead to profit as surely as haste leads to poverty."

- **Proverbs 21:20:** "The wise store up choice food and olive oil, but fools gulp theirs down."

- **Luke 14:28:** "Suppose one of you wants to build a tower. Won't you first sit down and estimate the cost?"

- **Ecclesiastes 11:2 (NIV):** "Invest in seven ventures, yes, in eight; you do not know what disaster may come upon the land."

- **1 Timothy 6:17-19 (NIV):** "Command those who are rich in this present world not to be arrogant nor to put their hope in wealth, which is so uncertain, but to put their hope in God, who richly provides us with everything for our enjoyment. Command them to do good, to be rich in good deeds, and to be generous and willing to share."

- **Proverbs 22:7 (NIV):** "The borrower is slave to the lender."

- **1 Corinthians 4:2 (NASB):** "In this case, moreover, it is required of stewards that one be found trustworthy."

Proverbs 21:5 highlights the importance of thoughtful and diligent planning, and Proverbs 21:20 emphasizes saving for the future and living wisely in the present. We also observe the principle behind mutual funds in Ecclesiastes 11:2. Assets must be diversified to reduce risk.

Jesus Himself, who worked as a carpenter, taught practical wisdom in financial matters. In Luke 14:28, He said, "Suppose one of you wants to build a tower. Won't you first estimate the cost to see if you have enough money to complete it?" This is a reminder that financial planning is a matter of common sense, something even the secular world recognizes. Jesus understood the importance of counting costs in construction and every area of life, including finances.

When we do not count the cost and borrow way beyond our means, debt enslaves us, and such bondage feels as it describes: we are slaves (Proverbs 22:7). This is why in principle, 1 Corinthians 4:2 prizes the call to be faithful stewards of the resources God has given us. Faithfulness in financial matters is not optional; it's a clear biblical mandate. When we are not, we cannot "be generous...[or] willing to share" (1 Timothy 6:19).

The Pitfall of Living Beyond Your Means

Despite the apparent wisdom of financial prudence, many Christians fall into the trap of living beyond their means. I've seen this all too often in couples—especially younger ones—buying their first home or upgrading to a larger house. They stretch their budget, rationalizing that they can afford it because it's their "dream house." In their excitement, they overlook the long-term financial implications, thinking they can manage. They work the numbers to fit their desires, convincing themselves everything will work out. But months later, reality sets in. Unexpected expenses arise, credit card debt piles up, and soon, they're drowning in financial obligations.

The initial joy of buying that dream home is quickly replaced by stress, arguments, and financial panic. He has to take a second job, and she considers running a daycare out of the house to make ends meet. All the while, their vision of hosting Bible studies or reaching out to neighbors gets shelved. Instead of being a testimony to

God's provision, they become an example of poor decision-making.

Have you ever heard such comments?

> "Buying our dream house proved to be a nightmare."

> "Our forever home became our forever debt."

> "What we thought would be a little heaven on earth feels like a little bit of hell."

> "A month after signing, we looked at each other in regret and asked, 'What have we done?'"

> "We believed this investment was wise and in our best interests, but now we struggle to pay the interest."

> "We believed this home was a blessing from God, but now we're questioning if we heard Him right."

> "Our 'once-in-a-lifetime opportunity' has become a lifetime of regret."

Bad stewardship undermines ministry. There must be a delay in gratification; otherwise, we will become lopsided on the 3 S's. We must save, spend, and share, not just spend, spend, spend. When we neglect saving and sharing, we hinder our ability to bless others and honor God's purposes. We cannot rescue others who need the Savior when we are drowning in debt. Yes, God will use us despite ourselves, but it's not easy to do if we are controlled by fear, stress, and financial bondage. To be effective vessels for His work, we must first find freedom in our lives. When we manage our resources wisely, we are better equipped to serve, give, and fulfill the purposes He has set before us. True stewardship is about aligning our financial choices with God's calling, ensuring we are prepared to help others and advance His kingdom, unburdened and unafraid.

How painful to imagine your unbelieving friends making the following comments in light of your lack of financial stewardship?

> "If your God can't help you manage your finances, how is He going to help me with my problems?"

> "You talk about the peace of Christ, but all I see is anxiety and fear over your bills."

> "How can I trust your advice about spiritual matters when your marriage is falling apart over your spending addiction?"

> "I thought Christians were supposed to live differently, but your financial mess looks just like everyone else's."

"You say you trust God, but your life seems just as stressed out and chaotic as mine!"

The Impact on Our Witness

This kind of financial strain doesn't stay hidden. Neighbors see the couple struggling and hear the arguments. Their children feel the stress in the home, and instead of seeing the peace that should come from living within their means, they witness financial chaos. It's hard to convince an unbeliever that following Christ brings joy and peace when they see Christians making unwise financial decisions.

Financial stress impacts every area of their lives when Christians are burdened by financial stress. They are often too exhausted to attend church, much less engage in ministry or outreach. Their once bright vision of hosting small groups or reaching their neighbors fades under the weight of financial strain. Instead of reflecting Christ's peace and provision, they are consumed by arguments, stress, and panic. The joy they hoped to spread is overshadowed by their financial reality.

When Christians fail to manage their resources wisely, it shows a lack of responsibility and can damage their witness. Even the secular world understands the importance of living within your means and avoiding debt. They know what it looks like to count the cost, and when they see Christians who don't follow these basic principles, it sends a message that is anything but appeal-

Proverbs 21:20 advises, "The wise store up choice food and olive oil, but fools gulp theirs down."

ing. Why would an unbeliever seek counsel from a Christian on spiritual matters if that Christian can't even manage their finances?

As Scripture declares, "The borrower becomes the lender's slave." When Christians are enslaved by debt due to unwise spending, it's difficult to point others to the freedom found in Christ. It often pushes people away. I have never heard a banker say to a nearly bankrupt Christian couple, "What church do you attend? Because of you, I want to visit some Sunday morning." Financial mismanagement doesn't attract people to Christ; it repels them.

And let's be clear: I'm not referring to those who experience unforeseen tragedies, such as a child's illness that leads to financial hardship or losing a job unexpectedly. These are situations beyond anyone's control, and the world acknowledges that. I'm talking about Christians who knowingly make impulsive, irresponsible decisions—buying homes or making large purchases they can't afford—and then wonder why they end up in financial ruin. To them, a penny earned is two pennies spent. When the math doesn't add up, and we knowingly live beyond our means, we hurt ourselves, our families, and our testimony for Christ.

One great example of financial prudence comes from Dave Ramsey, a man whose life story reflects how God's wisdom can turn financial ruin into a platform for teaching others. Early in his career, Ramsey built a successful real estate portfolio, only to lose it all and declare bankruptcy in his twenties. Rather than crumbling under financial pressure, Ramsey turned to biblical financial management principles. He rebuilt his life through hard work, budgeting, and smart investments, ultimately founding Financial Peace University to help others avoid the same financial pitfalls.

Ramsey's recovery from financial collapse shows how faith and perseverance can turn financial loss into a testimony of God's wisdom and provision. Today, his teachings on avoiding debt, living on a budget, and saving for the future have helped millions of people manage their money wisely. His example is a powerful testimony of how following biblical financial principles can restore one's economic health and lead to a greater spiritual impact.

Practical Applications for Financial Stewardship

So what should we do to ensure that our financial lives align with biblical principles and provide a strong witness to the world? Here are a few practical applications:

Create a Budget: Establish a budget that reflects your income, expenses, and savings goals. Stick to it, and avoid making impulsive purchases that could jeopardize your financial stability. One couple said, "We were drowning in debt and constantly stressed about money. That's when we decided to sit down and create a budget together. For the first time, we tracked every dollar we earned and spent, prioritizing our debt payments and cutting unnecessary expenses. It wasn't easy, but sticking to that budget changed everything. We stopped making impulsive purchases, and every month, we saw our debt shrinking. Instead of feeling overwhelmed, we're in control of our finances and working as a team towards a debt-free future."

Save for the Future: As Proverbs 21:20 advises, "The wise store up choice food and olive oil, but fools gulp theirs down." Save consistently for future needs, emergencies, and retirement. A lack of savings can lead to financial panic when unexpected events occur. I have heard this testimony, which should give all of us hope. "I used to spend every penny I earned, convinced that I would always be able to handle whatever came my way. But when an unexpected medical emergency hit, I realized how unprepared I was. With no savings to fall back on, I found myself in a financial crisis. That's when I turned to Proverbs 21:20 and started saving consistently. Little by little, I built up an emergency fund and began contributing to my retirement. Now, instead of living in fear of what could go wrong, I have a sense of peace knowing I'm prepared for the future. Saving has become a discipline that not only protects me but also honors God's wisdom."

On a personal note, when I became a senior pastor at 29, several board members advised me to start a savings program. At the time, I didn't see the urgency but didn't oppose the idea either. I understood its wisdom but felt I had plenty of time before I needed to worry about retirement, which seemed four decades away. However, they respectfully disagreed and allocated part of my income to be set aside for retirement. Forty years later, an individual overseeing that account approached me and said, "You're now at the age to access the funds that have been accumulating over these four decades." I had not kept track of that account and barely remembered it existed. But as some say, the world's eighth wonder is compound interest, and I fully agree. When I inquired about the amount, I was so shocked by the figure that I nearly fell out of my chair. As the saying goes, "Save more than you spend." When you do this consistently for 40 years, the interest alone on your principal can grow to an astounding sum. Even Jesus acknowledged the principle of earning interest in Luke 19:23, where He said, "Why then did you not put my money in the bank, and having come, I would have collected it with interest?"

Avoid Debt: Avoid accumulating debt, especially through credit cards or loans for items that aren't necessities. If you're already in debt, create a plan to pay it down as quickly as possible. Dave Ramsey hears this testimony constantly. "I used to swipe my credit card for everything, thinking it was no big deal as long as I made the minimum payments. But soon, I found myself buried under a mountain of debt. I felt trapped and overwhelmed, as if I was working just to pay interest. That's when I realized what Proverbs 22:7 meant: 'The borrower becomes the lender's slave.' I knew I had to break free. I stopped using my credit cards, created a strict repayment plan, and committed to paying down my debt as quickly as possible. It wasn't easy, but every payment was a step toward freedom. Today, I'm debt-free and determined to live within my means, no longer a slave to debt. We visited Dave Ramsey in Nashville to shout out that we are debt-free."

Live Within Your Means: Don't be like the person who exclaimed, "We are determined to live within our means even if we have to borrow to do so!" Be content with what you have, and resist the temptation to live beyond your means. Your lifestyle should reflect financial prudence, not extravagance. Living simply can be a powerful testimony to those around you. This represents many: "I was constantly trying to keep up with the Joneses—buying the latest gadgets, wearing designer clothes, and driving a luxury car. I thought having these things would make me feel successful, but instead, it was killing me financially and emotionally. I was drowning in debt and stress, all for the sake of appearances. One day, I decided to stop competing and comparing. I realized it wasn't worth the cost. I scaled back, focused on what truly mattered, and found contentment in living within my means. Letting go of that endless competition gave me the peace I had been searching for all along. I also discovered that people didn't like me any more, or any less."

Encouragement in Financial Prudence

A friend once said something that deeply impacted me: "If an unbeliever sees that we cannot make good decisions regarding our money, why would they trust our decision-making if they seek counsel regarding issues in their own lives?"

The secular world recognizes the importance of stewarding our finances, and so should we as Christians. How we manage our money reflects our faith, wisdom, and self-discipline. When we live within our means, save for the future, and avoid unnecessary debt, we create a platform for having the energy and mental space to share the peace and provision of Christ with others.

FOUR

Valuing Time
(Time Is Money)

Sarah and I have prayed over this Scripture since early in our marriage: "So teach us to number our days, That we may present to You a heart of wisdom" (Psalm 90:12). We understood the importance of valuing time for a lifetime as a precious resource. We have never said this morbidly, but we kept before us this fact: we will die. We only have so much time. Additionally, Ecclesiastes 3:1 tells us, "For everything there is a season and a time for every matter under heaven." Recognizing the right time for everything helps us align our actions with God's purposes. Furthermore, Proverbs 21:5 warns, "Everyone who is hasty comes only to poverty." This verse cautions against rushing through life without proper planning and reflection.

The world values productivity and time management. They interpret this as under the umbrella of stewardship. They expect of themselves and Christians to steward their time wisely—not just money. Poor time management impairs productivity and undermines our witness before unbelievers, who find this inconsistency troubling. Seeing believers failing to manage their time effectively raises doubts about our ability to live out the principles we profess. Effective time management, therefore, is not just about personal efficiency but also about showcasing the integrity and diligence that reflect Christ's lordship in every area of our lives.

Scripture echoes this sentiment in Ephesians 5:15-16, which reads: "Look carefully then how you walk, not as unwise but as wise, making the best use of the time, because the days are evil." This reminds us that our time should be used wisely and purposefully to reflect God's priorities.

The Bible teaches the importance of using our time wisely because time is one of the most precious resources God has given us. When Christians fail to use their time wisely, are seen wasting it, or run around hastily, unable to be present, this can undermine their testimony, making it difficult for unbelievers to view their faith as meaningful or transformative.

Could any of these statements represent you and your stewardship of time?

"I used to show up late to everything, making others wait on me, and I realized my lack of punctuality was not only rude but also a poor reflection of Christ's love and respect for others."

"Constantly running from one thing to the next left me stressed and easily annoyed, snapping at my family and friends, and I knew I needed to slow down and manage my time better to reflect God's peace."

"I was so busy doing things for the King that I had no time with the King, and it took a toll on my spiritual life and relationship with God, forcing me to reevaluate my priorities."

"In my hurry to get things done, I made hasty decisions that led to serious mistakes, and I realized I needed to slow down and seek God's guidance instead of rushing through life."

"Mismanaging my time at work led to poor performance, and seeing my colleagues produce more with the same hours convicted me to steward my time more wisely and honor my role with integrity."

These testimonies address lateness, stress, spiritual neglect, hasty decisions, integrity, and workplace performance, highlighting the consequences of poor time management and the need for change.

Among working people and parents, no one in the world argues against the idea that productivity, lower stress, and a better quality of life come from wise time management. Everyone favors intelligent prioritization, planning, and managing time based on personal values and long-term benefits. Time management isn't about rigidity; it's about making the most of our days in a way that reflects our goals and priorities.

Think About the Hours We Have In a Week

Here's a typical breakdown:

Total Hours in a Week
7 days x 24 hours = 168 hours

Subtracting Essential Activities:

Sleep: 8 hours per night x 7 days = 56 hours

Work: 8 hours x 5 days per week + 1 hour x
5 days per week for commuting = 45 hours

Eating and Personal Care:
2 hours per day x 7 days per week = 14 hours

Total Subtracted Essential Time:
56 hours (sleep) + 45 hours (work and commute) +
14 hours (eating and personal care) = 115 hours

Discretionary (Free) Time:
168 total hours - 115 essential hours =
53 hours of free time per week

This means that after accounting for sleep, work, and basic daily activities, an average person has about 53 hours each week for other activities such as family, hobbies, exercise, relaxation, or additional responsibilities. Of course, this will vary based on individual schedules and commitments, but it provides a general framework for understanding how our time is distributed.

How do you spend your 53 hours?

We often claim to be too busy, yet when we break it down, we have more discretionary hours than we realize. Are we using those hours effectively, or are they wasted on things that don't align with our true priorities? Have we overfilled them, leading to an overwhelmed, un-present schedule?

It's time to take an honest look at how we're spending our time and ask ourselves if we're stewarding it in a way that honors God and fulfills our purpose. Time is money… but time is more valuable than money.

As a college student, I wasn't making much money, but I discovered that using my time wisely could achieve things of great value. I realized I could be more productive by planning all my assignments on a large calendar. I would list every due date for papers and exams and then work backward, estimating how much time each task would take. I would set a start date and draw a line to the deadline, showing what I needed to work on each day.

To my surprise, sticking to this schedule gave me abundant free time. Despite my heavy workload, I had time to do so much more than study and write. It was truly eye-opening. Organizing my time boosted my productivity and created space for additional activities I enjoyed. Managing my time effectively profited me in ways I never imagined.

Wasting Time and Poor Time Management

Time is a valuable resource, and managing it well prevents the waste of energy and potential. We are running a race and must manage our time wisely to run well for a lifetime. Too many people say, "I wasted my life doing things that didn't matter to the Lord." We need to value time to prevent this.

Consider how damaging it can be when believers demonstrate poor time management in the workplace. Take, for example, a young seminarian who worked at a local coffee shop while studying for ministry. His duties were straightforward: opening early, greeting customers, and making drinks. But he often arrived late, leaving a line of irritated commuters waiting for their morning coffee. When the remote workers came in for their bottomless drip coffee and to set up for the afternoon, he would often be found leaning against the counter, scrolling through his phone, oblivious to the customers waiting at the register. Later, he struggled to gain credibility when he attempted to start a church in the same community. People were hesitant to believe that someone with such poor work habits would have the reliability to lead a church successfully.

Let's consider the believer who isn't lazy but simply overwhelmed by the demands of life. This individual constantly feels frazzled, disorganized, and unable to meet responsibilities. When asked by a non-Christian friend how they are doing, they routinely respond, "I'm stressed out." This lack of organization may not be intentional, but it still causes them to appear unreliable and incapable of handling life's pressures. Their ongoing stress becomes a message to unbelievers that something is missing—Christians are meant to carry peace and balance, not constant anxiety.

Imagine how damaging it is when this believer is supposed to pick up someone's child from school and forgets or shows up late, causing panic for the parents and child. This type of disorganization, though unintentional, can discredit a believer's ability to serve others effectively. It leaves non-believers wondering what value Christ brings to a person's life if they can't manage their time correctly.

The lazy time-waster and the frazzled individual struggling with disorganization send the wrong message to those around them. We are called to reflect Christ in all areas of our lives, and poor time management limits our ability. Failing to show up on time or missing deadlines can frustrate the people around us, especially unbelievers who may have expected more from a Christian.

Time is a gift from God, and we must steward it well as believers. When we fail to do so, it impacts our ability to serve effectively and limits God's potential to use us in greater ways. Furthermore, poor time management affects our relationships and the witness we present to non-believers, whether it's at work, with family, or in our communities.

Time is a gift from God, and we must steward it well as believers. When we fail to do so, it impacts our ability to serve effectively and limits God's potential to use us in greater ways. Furthermore, poor time management affects our relationships and the witness we present to non-believers, whether it's at work, with family, or in our communities.

Practical Applications for Valuing Time

How can we, as Christians, develop better time management habits to reflect the wisdom and diligence that Christ calls us to? Here are a few practical steps:

Set Priorities: Identify what is most important in your life and organize your time accordingly. Matthew 6:33 reminds us to "seek first the kingdom of God," meaning that our time should reflect our pursuit of God's priorities. This comment I received represents some of us. "I spent years saying yes to everything, thinking busyness equaled productivity. When I asked God to help me set priorities, I learned to say no to good things and yes to the best things, and my life became more meaningful and focused."

Use a Schedule or Planner: Whether it's a digital calendar or a physical planner, writing down appointments, responsibilities, and deadlines can keep you on track and help you avoid over-committing. When the *Franklin Planner* first came out, Sarah and I embraced it wholeheartedly. For years, it was our go-to tool for organizing our busy lives. It helped us manage our time and tangibly set goals and priorities. There was something powerful about putting pen to paper and seeing our commitments before us. It taught us to be intentional with our time, ensuring we align our daily schedules with God's purposes. Whether you use a traditional planner or a digital tool, the key is to have a system that allows you to steward your time effectively and avoid the trap of overcommitment.

Avoid Procrastination: Proverbs 6:9-11 warns against laziness, urging us to consider the ways of the ant, which stores provisions and works steadily. Avoid delaying tasks by breaking them into smaller, manageable pieces. A family member told me, "I used to put off everything, from work deadlines to household chores, always telling myself I'd get to it later. This habit started in my younger days when I thrived on a 'do or die' mentality—waiting until the last minute to pull an all-nighter, believing my intensity and attentiveness were at their peak under pressure. However, that pattern later led to dropping the ball since too many other responsibilities prevented this last-minute strategy. When I began calendaring earlier, creating smaller tasks, and staying on task, I countered that tendency to procrastinate and have accomplished more with less anxiety."

Learn to Say No: Recognize your limits and be willing to say "no" to things that don't align with your top priorities. Years ago, this simple truth hit me hard: when you keep saying "yes" to everyone, you are saying "no" to someone - usually a family member. People pleasers end up displeasing the people who matter. Can you identify with this person? "I used to say yes to everything—work projects, church events, and social gatherings—because I didn't want to disappoint anyone. But I ended up exhausted and feeling resentful. I eventually realized that others understand when we say 'no' because we have other responsibilities, and their level of disappointment was far less than I had imagined. I also realized I said 'yes' too often so that others would value and like me, and then I'd feel significant. When I learned to say no and set boundaries, I found the freedom to focus on what truly mattered, and my relationships became more meaningful and peaceful." Jesus often withdrew to quiet places to rest and pray though the crowds' needs remained ever present (Luke 5:16), showing us that rest and boundaries are important.

Delegate When Appropriate: Exodus 18:13-26 recounts the advice Moses received from Jethro, telling him to delegate tasks to others to avoid burnout. Sometimes, managing time wisely means sharing the load with others. This person discovered: "I used to think I had to do everything myself because I believed no one could do it as well as I could. My perfectionism led to burnout, stress, and missing precious time with my family. I was afraid to delegate, but when I finally let go, others stepped up eagerly and even did things better than I could. When I entrusted them with responsibility, people felt valued and appreciated, and I discovered their unique strengths. Letting go didn't mean losing control; it meant empowering others and finding balance in my own life."

Reflect and Adjust: Periodically review how you're using your time and make adjustments as needed. Ephesians 5:15-16 calls us to "make the most of every opportunity," and sometimes that means reevaluating how we spend our days. My daughter Joy and her husband Matt have adopted this principle beautifully. Every week, they review their schedules for the next week, discuss any to-do's that went undone in the previous week, and pray over the upcoming agenda. Then, annually and sometimes bi-annually, they set aside a day or two, away from their three young kids, to make a retreat of reflection, setting goals, prayer, realigning their priorities, and thinking about the end of their lives and if they are living in a way now that aligns with how they want their children to speak about them at their funeral. This intentional time of reflection and planning helps them stay focused and connected, ensuring they're not just busy but purposefully investing their time in what truly matters. By taking a step back to evaluate, they ensure their actions align with their values and God's direction for their family. This practice of regular reflection and adjustment has brought them greater peace, strengthened their marriage, and allowed them to pursue their goals with clarity and intention.

You Can Be Like This

Time is one of God's most valuable gifts, and how we use it reflects our understanding of stewardship and our commitment to His calling on our lives. Whether we struggle with laziness or feel overwhelmed by life's demands, we need God's guidance in using our time wisely.

Here are testimonies of people who recognized the value of time and, over time, experienced great things:

> "I used to feel constantly overwhelmed and behind. Then I started using a planner and prioritizing my time. Now, I'm able to manage my business efficiently and still make it to all my kids' games. Taking control of my time has strengthened my relationship with my family."

> "I was always running late and missing deadlines. I realized it was affecting my job and my witness. I committed to managing my time better, using a daily schedule. Now, I'm more productive at work, and I've earned the respect of my colleagues, who have seen the change in my life."

> "I used to say yes to everything and ended up exhausted and resentful. Learning to say no and set boundaries was life-changing. Now, I'm less stressed and more focused on what truly matters. It's amazing how much more I can give when I'm not stretched too thin."

> "I was always the last to arrive and the first to leave events, missing opportunities to connect with others. When I started valuing my time and planning my days, I began showing up early and engaging more. This change opened doors for meaningful relationships and ministry opportunities I never had before."

Poor time management doesn't just hurt us—it affects our relationships, our effectiveness in serving others, and our witness to the unbelieving world. As we grow in our ability to manage time well, we can better reflect the peace, balance, and purpose that come from living a life grounded in Christ.

FIVE

Originality in Problem-Solving
(Think Outside the Box)

You don't need to be a genius to think outside the box—anyone can do it! It's about being open to new ways of approaching big or small challenges. Whether finding a creative solution to a problem at work, helping a neighbor uniquely, or trying a different approach to a personal goal, thinking outside the box simply means looking beyond the usual and daring to try something different. You can make a positive impact right where you are with courage and imagination. Remember, sometimes, the smallest, simplest ideas can have the greatest effect! When we feel stuck or unsure, we can ask God for wisdom, as promised in James 1:5, and trust that He will guide us with fresh ideas and solutions. Embracing this mindset allows us to see new possibilities, solve problems effectively, and serve others meaningfully.

The secular world values creativity and problem-solving, especially when these lead to tangible benefits for others. Those who think outside the box are often rewarded and recognized in business, education, and healthcare.

When I Thought Outside the Box

Traditionally, marriage books and counseling have often been directed toward women under the assumption that they are more interested in the subject and more likely to seek help. However, as a pastor studying Scripture, I saw nothing in the Bible to suggest that women are the only ones concerned with marriage. This prompted me to think outside the publishing paradigm and question these traditional assumptions, especially when my publisher told me to write *Love & Respect* to wives since they bought marriage books. I replied, "Could that be because you keep telling authors who write marriage books to slant the book in favor of wives?"

Ironically, the common belief that men are indifferent to marriage issues and that they are the primary problem has led many men to avoid seeking marriage help or counseling altogether, and they feel like the books label them as the primary problem. Over the years, I've spoken with many counselors and asked them a simple question: "If I could tell you how to get men to line up outside your office, would you want to know?"

The truth is, the responsibility of marriage doesn't rest solely with men any more than it does with women. The ground at the foot of the cross is level. Scripture does not teach that men are inherently unteachable while women are naturally receptive. Both men and women have needs, vulnerabilities, and teachability. The real challenge for teachers and counselors is to understand what truly softens, motivates, and empowers both men and women so that both want to pursue help and change.

From conducting live, two-day marriage conferences with an average attendance of 1,800 people, our surveys at Love and Respect Ministries consistently showed that 49% of those who initiated attending were husbands. This completely counters the narrative that men are disinterested in marriage. This supported my original thought with my publisher—who says only women want to improve their marriage? When writing the book, I took my Biblical hypothesis into account, ignoring the publisher's suggestion and thinking outside the box. I wanted to try to solve the problem of marital issues in a new way. So, I wrote to women and men, and what were the results? Men heard their "mother tongue" and responded well (and the book sold 100,000 hardcover copies in three months and won several awards).

Creative Approaches in Ministry: Learning from the Dream Center

One of the best examples of creative problem-solving in ministry is the Dream Center in Los Angeles. Founded by Pastor Matthew Barnett and his father, Tommy Barnett, the Dream Center began as a traditional church but quickly adapted to meet the pressing needs of its community. Their approach was revolutionary: instead of focusing solely on church services, they transformed their ministry into a community resource center, offering extensive outreach programs, including transitional housing, food banks, medical clinics, and more. I have had the privilege of speaking there two times. It is incredible.

During my time speaking at the Dream Center in LA, I found the foundation's mission encapsulated in its motto, "Find a need and fill it; find a hurt and heal it."[3] Their innovative ministry model involves looking beyond the traditional church setting to address the physical, emotional, and spiritual needs of those they serve. They saw the struggles of the homeless, the addicted, and the marginalized, and rather than turning a blind eye, they chose to be a light in the darkness. This kind of ministry requires boldness, creativity, and perseverance—qualities that reflect Christ's heart for all people.

During the COVID-19 pandemic, the Dream Center adapted its operations to serve over 10,000 meals daily to struggling families. This was not an easy feat, but it demonstrated the center's commitment to being flexible and responsive to the needs around it. Their efforts didn't go unnoticed—several secular organizations partnered with them because of their effectiveness and adaptability, showcasing Christ's love in action through practical service.

The Dream Center's success has drawn attention from various sectors, including partnerships with secular organizations and foundations. Its impact has been so profound that even those outside the faith have been drawn to its work, seeing the tangible love of Christ in action. This relentless problem-solving and commitment to service are powerful witnesses, proving that the church can be a force for good in every community.

The Dream Center's story shows perseverance and creative problem-solving can lead to remarkable practical and spiritual outcomes. Their willingness to adapt and find innovative solutions has not only improved countless lives but also served as a powerful witness to the transformative power of Christ.

What the Scripture Says on Problem-Solving

The following verses encourage us to use wisdom and discernment in our choices and decisions, which may require us to step outside our comfort zones and find creative solutions that better serve others. However, these solutions are readily available to us, and God can give us tools to become discerning, creative, and sharp.

- **Ecclesiastes 10:10 (NIV):** "If the ax is dull and its edge unsharpened, more strength is needed, but skill will bring success."

- **Proverbs 15:14:** "The mind of the intelligent seeks knowledge…"

- **Ecclesiastes 7:25:** "I directed my mind to know, to investigate, and to seek wisdom and an explanation…"

- **James 1:5 (NIV):** "If any of you lacks wisdom, you should ask God, who gives generously to all without finding fault, and it will be given to you."

- **Philippians 1:9-10:** "And this is my prayer: that your love may abound more and more in knowledge and depth of insight, so that you may be able to discern what is best."

- **Matthew 10:16 (NIV):** "I am sending you out like sheep among wolves. Therefore be as shrewd as snakes and as innocent as doves."

Testimonies of Problem Solving and How It Can Change Communities

The following stories draw on the common themes and struggles couples face. These are powerful testaments to the power of problem-solving. Many of us can look around our communities and easily come up with a laundry list of issues. If we found a solution to one of these small problems, what could that demonstrate to other non-believers? What could happen if Christians prayed to God for creative, wise ways to fulfill community needs? What if these became your testimony?

Turning Trash into Treasure: What if your small town faced a litter problem, and traditional clean-up efforts weren't making a lasting impact? Imagine starting an art project encouraging kids and families to collect trash and transform it into sculptures around town. This could become a community-wide event that cleans up the streets and instills pride and creativity in everyone involved. What if people began to see your church as a place that creatively cares for the environment, reflecting the beauty and redemption that Jesus brings to broken things?

Launching a "Cup with a Cop" Program: Consider starting a simple yet unconventional initiative to build trust between the police and your community, especially among youth. What if you organized weekly "Cup of Coffee with a Cop" events at local cafes, where officers and residents could talk informally? It could start small, but these conversations might lead to meaningful relationships and mutual understanding over time. Imagine people saying, "I see them as people now, not just uniforms." Could your church become known as a bridge-builder in your community?

Faith and Fitness: What if you combined the separate elements of faith and fitness at your church into one program? You could start a "Faith and Fitness" class, incorporating prayer, worship music, and Scripture meditation into workouts. At first, people might be skeptical, but imagine the potential for growth as participants experience physical and spiritual transformation. Could this unique class attract people from the community who wouldn't typically attend church, becoming a powerful outreach tool?

The Secular World Applauds Critical and Caring Thinking

The secular world often leads to innovative thinking, creating solutions to complex problems through technology, medicine, and humanitarian work. Even though profit may motivate some of these innovations, the underlying desire to improve lives and care for people in new ways cannot be denied. When Christians are seen as resistant to change or stuck in tradition, it can be a turnoff to unbelievers, leading them to question the authenticity and relevance of our faith.

A significant example occurred during the Houston flooding when Lakewood Church, a mega church in the area, came under fire for not initially opening its doors as a shelter. The church faced backlash on social media for what was perceived as a lack of care. While they later clarified that the building was temporarily inaccessible due to severe flooding and that they were coordinating with city officials, the initial reaction was swift and harsh. This incident highlights how quickly public perception can turn negative when people believe that Christians aren't willing to think outside the box or take immediate action in times of crisis.

Some of the same issues arose with Samaritan's Purse. During the COVID-19 pandemic we observed a prime example of thinking outside the box. Setting up a mobile hospital in Central Park, New York City, provided crucial support to overwhelmed hospitals. Despite facing criticism, their efforts were a lifeline for many. This response demonstrated that when believers step up in creative, compassionate ways, it resonates deeply with people, even those who might otherwise be skeptical of Christianity.

Many churches and Christians resist change, falling into the trap of thinking, "We've never done it that way before." These are what I like to call "The Seven Last Words of the Church." This mindset can be detrimental, especially when it prevents us from creatively solving problems or serving others in new ways. It communicates that the Church isn't open to considering alternatives or trying new things, perhaps out of fear, and the cost becomes showing Christ's love in tangible ways. Believers need to break free from tradition when necessary and seek new ways to care for the world around them.

Practical Applications for Creative and Caring Thinking

Seek God's Wisdom: Proverbs 2:6 says, "For the Lord gives wisdom; from his mouth come knowledge and understanding." Spend time in prayer, asking God for guidance in thinking creatively and finding new ways to serve others. Someone shared, "When the pandemic hit, my small business was on the verge of collapse. I had exhausted all my options and felt completely lost. One night, I knelt down and prayed, asking God for wisdom and direction. An idea that seemed impossible came to mind— shifting my retail business to an online platform overnight. I felt an unusual peace and decided to go for it. I sought help from others and learned new skills, and within months, my business was not only surviving but thriving. God's wisdom guided me through what seemed like an insurmountable challenge."

Be Willing to Change: Don't be afraid to break away from traditional methods if they are no longer effective. Jesus Himself challenged traditions when they hindered true worship and cared for others. This person shared such a shift. "I used to think evangelism meant handing out tracts and having debates, but it wasn't working. People were put off, and I felt discouraged. After praying for guidance, I felt led to just start listening to people's stories and being a friend. I stopped pushing and started caring. It was a slow process, but I built genuine relationships. A few years later, several of those friends gave their lives to Christ because they saw something different in me. I learned that sometimes, changing our approach is what's needed to truly share the love of Jesus."

Look for Unmet Needs: Identify areas of need that others have overlooked. Like the Dream Center, seek out opportunities to serve in ways that address the unique challenges in your community. This person had great insight: "Everyone in our church was focused on supporting those who were sick, but I noticed that the caregivers—the spouses, parents, and children—were exhausted and isolated. I started a monthly support group just for them, where they could share their struggles and receive encouragement. One caregiver broke down in tears, saying, 'I didn't know anyone noticed what I'm going through.' Meeting this overlooked need brought healing and strength to those who were carrying the heaviest burdens."

Involve Others: Collaboration often leads to the best ideas. Work with others, ask for input, and partner with different groups to find solutions to challenging problems. I love what this person shared: "Our neighborhood was plagued by crime and neglect, and I felt overwhelmed trying to make a difference on my own. I decided to start a community meeting, inviting local businesses, schools, and residents to brainstorm solutions together. At first, only a few showed up, but as we kept meeting, more people got involved. We created a neighborhood watch, organized clean-up events, and even started a tutoring program for kids. Over time, crime rates dropped, and our neighborhood became more optimistic about the future. Working together, we accomplished what none of us could have done alone."

Anticipate Criticism, but Stay the Course: Criticism may come even when doing the right thing. Stay focused on your calling, trusting that your efforts will bear fruit in God's timing. As a pastor, I relate to this testimony. "As a new pastor, I felt led to implement changes in our church's structure to better serve our community. Some long-time members were furious, accusing me of ruining traditions and splitting the congregation. It was painful, and I often questioned myself. But I knew God had called me to lead in this way. I stayed committed, prayed for guidance, and continued the work. Slowly, the church began to grow, and new members, who were once hesitant, became active participants. One elderly member later confessed, 'I was wrong to resist. I see now that these changes brought life back to our church.'"

The Challenge for Believers: How Will You Respond?

As Christians, we are called to care for others with creativity and wisdom. The world is watching and often quicker to notice when we fail than when we succeed. However, stepping up and serving in innovative, selfless ways creates an undeniable impact.

Is there a situation in your life where you could think creatively and care for someone in a new way? How might your unbelieving friends respond if they saw you go above and beyond what is expected, sacrificing your time, resources, or comfort for the sake of others? This doesn't need to apply to your community or close family or friends. We often overlook the people closest to us, as there can be deep hurt and betrayal. Is there an opportunity to rethink how to solve a rift in your home, family, or close circle?

One person wrote: "My family had been torn apart by misunderstandings and grudges for years. Traditional attempts to reconcile, like family meetings and therapy sessions, weren't working. I decided to try something new: I organized a 'Family Memory Book' project, asking everyone to contribute their favorite memories and old photos. As we shared stories and compiled the book together, we began to see each other in a new light. Laughter replaced bitterness, and healing took place in a way I never thought possible. Sometimes, it takes a creative approach to mend what's broken."

As Christians, we are called to care for others with creativity and wisdom. The world is watching and often quicker to notice when we fail than when we succeed. However, stepping up and serving in innovative, selfless ways creates an undeniable impact.

Remember, God is the ultimate source of wisdom and creativity. If you feel stuck or unsure of how to move forward, turn to Him for guidance. James 1:5 reminds us that if we lack wisdom, we should ask God, who gives generously to all without finding fault.

Be encouraged if you've hesitated to step out of your comfort zone. God can use you in ways you may not even realize, and sometimes it starts with simply being willing to think outside the box and care for others in a new way.

SIX

Education for a Lifetime
(You're Never Too Old to Learn)

"At 72, I felt like life had passed me by. I had raised my kids, retired from my job, and felt there was nothing new left to learn. But then I joined a community Bible study group that encouraged us to dig deeper into the Word. I started studying Hebrew to understand the Scriptures better. It was challenging, but I felt alive again. My grandchildren were amazed to see me learning a new language at my age, and it opened up conversations about the Bible I never thought we'd have. This experience taught me that we're never too old to discover something new."

Christians should be known for their humility and willingness to grow. Proverbs 9:9 tells us that a wise person will become even wiser when they receive instruction, and a righteous person will increase in learning. Yet, many believers fall into complacency, mistakenly believing they've reached a point where they no longer need to learn. This kind of stagnation isn't just detrimental to personal spiritual growth—it damages our witness. When unbelievers see an aged Christian who has become closed-minded or unteachable, it sends a message that Christianity has no fresh relevance, no ongoing vibrancy.

Some people waste the opportunities before them by saying, "I'm too old" or "You can't teach an old dog new tricks," contrary to biblical teaching. Lifelong learning isn't just about formal education; it's about living each day actively seeking ways to grow in knowledge and wisdom. Scripture supports this. Proverbs 1:5 says, "Let the wise listen and add to their learning, and let the discerning get guidance." Ecclesiastes 4:13 also teaches, "Better a poor but wise youth than an old but foolish king who no longer knows how to heed a warning." Even the secular world recognizes the value of lifelong learning and understands the importance of being open to new knowledge and growth at any age.

I vividly remember a beloved professor in my church who deeply loved the Lord. His adult children recently shared a photo of him in his early 90s, taken just the day before he passed away. Seated at his desk with an open Bible, he was doing what he had done for decades—taking notes on what the Lord revealed. This lifelong practice of studying Scripture began in his twenties and continued until the day before his death. At his funeral,

I was struck by the profound image of him, early in the morning, faithfully reading his Bible - and within hours, he'd be dead. Ultimately, he sought to know God more intimately through His Word. This picture is permanently etched in my mind as a powerful testament to a life dedicated to learning who God is.

The secular world values lifelong learning and recognizes the importance of being open to education, new knowledge, and growth at any age. This principle of continual learning aligns with biblical wisdom. When Christians stop growing, they risk becoming stagnant and unrelatable, making their faith appear shallow and disconnected to believers and even to unbelievers.

Examples of Lifelong Learning

Over the years, I have heard or been sent countless testimonies from lifelong learners. I am encouraged by those who have decided to fight stagnation and continue learning, even when uncomfortable. While beneficial to the mind and spirit, it often was an opportunity for these learners to share their faith in a new way.

One widower shared: "After my wife passed away, I felt lost and unsure of how to navigate life without her. I realized I didn't even know how to cook for myself, let alone others. To cope with my loneliness, I decided to take a cooking class. As I learned to prepare gourmet meals, I found comfort in the kitchen and soon began inviting neighbors and new friends for dinner. These gatherings became opportunities to share good food, my faith, and the story of how God was helping me through my grief. One evening, a couple who had never been to church asked if they could join me on Sunday. What started as a way to fill the empty spaces in my life became a ministry of hospitality and connection, bringing new relationships and a sense of purpose I hadn't imagined possible."

A retired engineer said, "I was asked to mentor young professionals at my church. Initially, I thought I was there to teach them, but I ended up learning just as much from them. They introduced me to new technologies and perspectives that I had never considered. One young man said, 'Your willingness to learn from us, despite your experience, shows true humility.' Our mutual respect and growth made a lasting impact on the entire group."

Another said, "I joined a local book club, and I initially felt out of place, but as we discussed different books, I started sharing insights from my faith. People began asking more about my beliefs, and soon we were having deep discussions about God and life. One member told me, 'I always thought Christians were closed-minded, but you've shown me that faith can be thoughtful and open.' This new circle of friends became a place where I could share my faith naturally, all because I was willing to learn and engage in new conversations."

A history lover shared, "I enrolled in a world history course at the community college. I made new friends, and we often debated historical events and their impacts on today's world. One day,

A history lover shared, "I enrolled in a world history course at the community college. I made new friends, and we often debated historical events and their impacts on today's world. One day, I mentioned how my faith had shaped my perspective on history. That sparked a series of discussions where I could explain the influence of Christianity on various historical movements. My classmates appreciated my insights and even asked if I'd lead a study group on the history of Christianity."

I mentioned how my faith had shaped my perspective on history. That sparked a series of discussions where I could explain the influence of Christianity on various historical movements. My classmates appreciated my insights and even asked if I'd lead a study group on the history of Christianity."

Struggling to answer the tough questions about Christianity, this life-long learner sought answers. "I took an online course by Colson Fellows in apologetics, which gave me confidence and new tools to share my beliefs. I joined a debate group to practice, where I met many people with different viewpoints. One atheist member said, 'I appreciate that you're willing to have these conversations and listen.' We've continued our discussions outside the group, and while he hasn't come to faith yet, he now sees Christianity in a new, more positive light."

Why is being a lifelong learner critical for some churchgoers to hear?

Years ago, I remember hearing two Bible teachers express concern about the most carnal Christians they encountered—people who sat week after week listening to incredible Bible exposition. Yet, they failed to apply it to their lives. It's not that these Christians didn't hear the Word, but instead, they had become resistant to the conviction of the Holy Spirit. As a result, their hearts hardened, and they became unreachable and unteachable. Simultaneously, their testimony diminished. Of course, they didn't see this about themselves, but they resisted acting on a powerful sermon each week. They thought they were at the center of God's will because they heard something new and could talk about it. However, they had ears to hear but did not hear. Eyes to see but did not see.

These well-known Bible teachers pointed out how tragic it is when people who have been in the church for 30, 40, or 50 years can still show up each Sunday but stop learning and growing. Lifelong learning, especially for believers, means more than just hearing something new—it means applying that truth and allowing God to transform you. To be wise, we must continue to gain insight and wisdom, never believing we've "arrived" spiritually. By the way, new information just adds to our knowledge, and there is the potential that such "knowledge makes one conceited" (1 Corinthians 8:1), but new insight from Scripture should lead to personal application and change.

The Impact of a Humble, Teachable Spirit on Children

I have often observed that those fathers who came to Christ but remained teachable were some of the most impactful Christians I've known. These men would stand in the church lobby talking to others about where God had convicted them. They spoke humbly and honestly about where they needed to grow. What was striking about these moments was that their children were often nearby, watching and listening as their fathers confessed their need to continue growing and learning.

As the years passed, I noticed a powerful trend: many of these children, who had seen their fathers model humility and a teachable spirit, grew up to follow Christ with the same heartfelt conviction. By showing their children that learning and growth never stop in the Christian life, these fathers passed on not just the faith but the attitude of openness to God's ongoing work in their lives.

The Consequences of Stagnation

When non-believers see a Christian who refuses to learn or adapt, it discredits their testimony and isolates them from others. It can even discredit them to other believers looking to find role models and mentors in the faith. I know of a pastor who deeply loved God and His Word. He was committed to his congregation and excelled in teaching and shepherding his flock. However, he had a peculiar habit outside of the pulpit—during social gatherings and interactions with church members, he would try to be funny by imitating well-known comedians. Unfortunately, his attempts at humor were more awkward than amusing. People didn't laugh; instead, they felt uncomfortable and didn't know how to respond.

The church board, aware of the situation through multiple reports from members, decided to address this behavior directly. They approached the pastor with genuine concern, acknowledging his many strengths and expressing appreciation for his dedication. However, they gently pointed out that his efforts to be funny in social settings were not being received as he intended and were becoming a distraction. They asked him to refrain from this behavior, as it affected how people related to him and, ultimately, to his ministry.

To their surprise, the pastor seemed bewildered by their request. He couldn't understand why his attempts to lighten the mood were seen as problematic. He felt he was just trying to connect with people in a relaxed, informal way. Despite the board's kind and clear communication, he resisted change. He continued to behave the same way in social settings, believing that his intentions would eventually be understood and appreciated.

The board, increasingly frustrated and bewildered by his refusal to adjust his behavior, addressed the issue with him several more times. They expressed that his comedic attempts were not fostering the warm, welcoming environment he intended but instead were alienating people. The pastor, however, remained convinced that there was nothing wrong with his approach and that the board was overreacting.

After several warnings and much deliberation, the board reluctantly took more serious action. They explained to the pastor that despite repeated counsel, his unwillingness to listen and adapt damaged his credibility and effectiveness as a leader. If he did not change, they would have to consider asking him to step down from his role.

Heartbreakingly, the pastor did not heed their warnings. He continued with the same behavior, believing he was in the right. Eventually, the board had no choice but to let him go. His lack of teachability and unwillingness to change not only cost him his position but also deeply saddened those who had appreciated his many positive contributions to the church.

This story is a powerful reminder of the importance of humility and the willingness to accept feedback and continue learning, especially in ministry. No matter how dedicated or well-meaning we are, if we become resistant to change and fail to reevaluate our beliefs, even something as personal as how our behavior affects others, can undermine our effectiveness and the impact of our ministry. This pastor's story, though painful, highlights the need for every leader to remain teachable and open to growth for the sake of both their personal development and the health of the community they serve.

The Example of Humility in Lifelong Learning

On the other hand, consider the power of humility in lifelong learning. Colonel Sanders didn't start Kentucky Fried Chicken until his 60s. His willingness to learn, grow, and adapt, even in the later years of his life, is inspiring. Stories like these remind us that no matter how old we are, there's always more we can learn and ways to grow. Many do not know the following about Sanders:

Throughout his life, Sanders earned the reputation of having a temper and a penchant for coarse language, a vice which burdened his soul but one which he felt he had no control to remedy. Sanders confessed in his autobiography that his business success never gave him peace with God when his own tongue bore witness against him: "But all this while I knew I wasn't right with God. It bothered me especially when I'd take the name of the Lord in vain. I did my cussin' before women or anyplace. … I knew the terrible curse of cussin' would probably keep me out of heaven when I died." Sanders was 79 years old when he attended an evangelistic service at the Evangel Tabernacle in Louisville and prayed for Jesus Christ to save him from sin, gaining assurance of his salvation from Romans 10:9. On the day of his conversion, he also received counsel that God would help him clean up his foul speech, and five years later wrote that "when I asked the Lord to help me stop cussin' … I lost half of my vocabulary."[4]

The world respects those who remain humble and teachable, and this attitude can profoundly impact our witness. Imagine an elderly Christian deciding to go on a mission trip or volunteer in a new area of ministry. When they return and share stories of how they served and even helped lead someone to Christ, it's a powerful testimony of the work God is still doing in their life. Their willingness to learn and serve doesn't just speak to their personal growth—it speaks volumes to their unbelieving friends and family.

Consider this even during a tense election season or political debate. It might be tempting for those who have been around longer to claim they have "seen it all" and even know it all. While age does beget wisdom, and history tends to repeat itself, I challenge you to be open to what those younger than you are saying. What are their wants, hopes, and needs? How have they changed from the hot-button issues of your youth? What could you learn from the younger generations? While this might not change your mind on a topic, there's a more likely than not chance you'll learn something or see their point of view in a new way that could lead to a deeper and more meaningful conversation.

Practical Applications for Lifelong Learning

Remain Humble and Teachable: Stay open to learning new things no matter your age or how much you think you know. A teachable spirit speaks to the humility Christ calls us to embody and allows others to see Christ's work in us. A Vietnam War veteran had carried bitterness and anger for decades. A local pastor invited him to a Bible study on forgiveness, and though skeptical, he attended. Over months of study and discussion, he learned that forgiveness is a lifelong process. His openness to God's teaching brought healing to his heart and helped other veterans find peace. This man's journey showed that being teachable is not just about knowledge but about transforming our hearts and letting Christ's love shine through us.

Embrace Change When Necessary: Be willing to adapt when new knowledge or better methods come along, which was also covered in the chapter on adaptability. This doesn't mean compromising on core doctrine but staying open to change in practical areas like health, finances, or relationships. People respect those who continue to learn and grow rather than clinging to old, ineffective ways. A tough, no-nonsense corporate leader wrote in to share how when her company introduced emotional intelligence training, she initially dismissed it as fluff. But after attending a session, she saw how her leadership style had alienated her team. Embracing change, she committed to improving her empathy and communication. Her adjustment fostered a more positive work environment, earning her the respect and loyalty of her employees, and this was especially important since she would often have guest speakers, like her pastor, present topics around faith. However, until she changed, most of her employees showed no interest.

Be a Role Model for Younger Believers: Show younger generations that learning never stops. When younger believers see an older Christian continuing to grow in wisdom, it inspires them to do the same and even might make them feel more connected to you. Your example of humility and lifelong learning becomes a living testimony to the power of God's ongoing work. A long-standing church elder realized he had dismissed the ideas of younger members too quickly. In a church meeting, he publicly apologized and invited them to share more. His humility and willingness to change his attitude inspired the younger members to engage more actively, knowing their voices were valued. His example showed that humility and openness to change can bridge generational divides.

Use Learning as a Way to Serve: Lifelong learning isn't just for our benefit. It equips us to serve others more effectively. Whether mentoring, volunteering, or going on mission trips, the knowledge and wisdom you gain through learning can impact those around you. A retired banker saw many low-income families struggling during tax season. He trained as a volunteer tax preparer, learning the ins and outs of tax credits and deductions for low-income households. Knowing a great deal about money, even so, he pursued a new avenue to serve others. His efforts saved these families thousands of dollars each year, and his patient guidance relieved those overwhelmed by the process. His commitment to learning a new skill enabled him to serve his community in a powerful, practical way.

Lifelong Learning as a Witness

As I mentioned earlier, and you may know, the secular world deeply values ongoing education and personal growth. People are inspired by those who continue learning and adapting, especially in their later years. Imagine the unbeliever who remains open, teachable, and humble as they age. They're willing to learn new things, embrace change, and keep growing. Now, picture a Christian who, by contrast, becomes closed-minded, unteachable, and set in their ways. It's no surprise which person the world would find more appealing.

Lifelong learning doesn't mean we compromise on doctrine, but it does mean we remain open to change in areas like relationships, health, and practical wisdom. When unbelievers see us growing in wisdom and understanding, it reflects well on our professing faith. They begin to see that our faith isn't just about attending church or holding to traditions—it's about a living, dynamic relationship with God that continually transforms us.

The Challenge to Keep Learning

Proverbs 1:5 says, "Let the wise listen and add to their learning, and let the discerning get guidance." Even unbelievers value ongoing education and growth. Christians who stop learning become stagnant, making their faith appear shallow. When we remain humble and teachable, it sends a message that our faith is alive and growing.

How are you doing in this area? Are you still learning, or have you become stuck in your ways? Lifelong learning is not just a worldly value—it's a biblical principle. Proverbs calls us to be people who never stop growing and learning. What could you commit to becoming a "student" of this year?

Let's commit to being people who are always learning, growing, and open to what God wants to teach us. Whether in spiritual matters or practical life decisions, being a lifelong learner is one of the most powerful testimonies we can offer the world.

SEVEN

Work Ethic
(Rome Wasn't Built in a Day)

Many of us look at others and think the grass is greener on their side of the fence. We believe that good fortune comes to certain people and not to us. But if their grass is greener, it may be because they're taking better care of it! It's not just about opportunity but about diligent effort. What may hold us back isn't lack of opportunity or ability, but sometimes, it's doing nothing with what we have in front of us. A person asked, "Isn't Joe lucky?" The reply was, "Yeah, and the harder he works, the luckier he gets."

Often, we avoid facing the truth and call our inactivity by another name. We are like the man who, after a medical examination, said to the doctor, "Give it to me straight, Doc. What's wrong with me?" The doctor replied, "You're just plain lazy." The man responded, "Okay, Doc. Now give me a scientific name for it so I can tell my wife."

Consistent hard work helps us accomplish worthy, lasting goals. When we work diligently, we see growth in our endeavors, whether in ministry, relationships, or personal development. Christians must reject shortcuts and embrace steady, hard work, which reflects diligence and honors God.

The world respects those who patiently build their success through discipline. As believers, we must embody this ethic, reflecting Christ's character through our dedication and perseverance in every area of life.

I've often joked with people that I'm not the smartest, most talented, wealthiest, or most popular—but I will be the one who attends your funeral! In other words, I'm a plodder. Like marathon runners, I pace myself. They don't sprint because if they do, they'll quit before reaching the finish line. Some people start fast, enthusiastically accepting every invitation and opportunity, but eventually, they burn out. They don't pace themselves well. Perhaps the idea is to start lightly jogging and never stop.

Truly, Rome Wasn't Built in a Day, and These Folks Grasped That

Similar to adaptability and resilience, work ethic requires determination and commitment. We may not reap what we sow immediately, but our determination and perseverance will be a

The world respects those who patiently build their success through discipline. As believers, we must embody this ethic, reflecting Christ's character through our dedication and perseverance in every area of life.

testimony to those around us. Read the following testimonies I share regarding the power of a strong work ethic.

Rising Above Poverty: "I grew up in a single-parent household, where every day was a struggle. My mother worked multiple jobs, and I often went to bed hungry. I knew that education was my way out. I studied hard, even when it meant missing out on social activities. It took years of sacrifice, but I earned a full scholarship and became the first in my family to graduate college. Today, I can support my mom and give back to my community. I see how God used every challenge to build my character and perseverance."

Building a Ministry from Scratch: "When I felt called to start a church in my small town, I had no resources or congregation. I spent months praying, knocking on doors, and hosting Bible studies in my living room. Attendance was often sparse, and I wondered if I was making any impact. But I kept trusting God and working diligently. Now, five years later, we have a thriving church community. God rewarded the slow, steady effort, and I've learned that true growth takes time and faith."

Overcoming Academic Struggles: "I've always struggled with learning disabilities, and school felt like an uphill battle. Every test and every assignment required twice the effort. My peers would breeze through material that took me hours to understand. But I didn't give up. I sought extra help, stayed up late studying, and pushed through my frustration. I graduated with honors and now work as a counselor, helping other students who face the same challenges I did. God showed me that persistence, not just talent, is key to success."

Restoring a Marriage: "My wife and I were on the brink of divorce. Years of neglect and unspoken resentment had built a wall between us. We decided to give it one last try, committing to counseling and daily prayer together. It was hard and uncomfortable, like learning to communicate all over again. But little by little, God healed our hearts. It wasn't an overnight transformation, but through persistent effort, we've rebuilt our marriage stronger than before."

Persevering Through a Creative Block: "As a writer, I've faced many seasons of creative drought where every word felt forced. There were times I considered quitting, thinking I had nothing left to offer. But I kept writing, even when the inspiration wasn't there. I wrote often, trusting that the flow would return. Now, I've published several books that have touched people's lives. God taught me that breakthroughs often come after long periods of perseverance."

Come Earlier, Leave Later: A business owner told me, "If an employee showed up 15 minutes before everyone else, and left 15 minutes after everyone else, I'd promote this person. The bar is set so low for some that this minimal effort just above mediocrity causes me to want to reward this person."

Diligent Effort vs. Overwork

Diligent effort is different from being a driven personality. It's not about working 12-16 hour days, rarely attending family functions, leaving early in the morning, and coming home after the kids are in bed. It's not focusing solely on winning at the expense of relationships or ignoring your spouse's needs. Because of Christ, diligent effort means persistently doing the work with a full heart, without idleness. It's not just working hard but working for Christ. Colossians 3:23-24 reads: "Whatever you do, do your work heartily, as for the Lord rather than for men; knowing that from the Lord you will receive the reward of the inheritance. It is the Lord Christ whom you serve."

One father shared, "I used to think that working hard meant putting in long hours at the office. But I was missing out on my kids' lives. After a wake-up call from my wife, I realized I needed to redefine my work ethic. I started prioritizing my time better, ensuring I was fully present at home. It wasn't easy to change my habits, but now, I'm not just successful in my career—I'm also a dad there for the little moments that matter. I've learned that diligent work includes building a strong family."

Similarly, Ephesians 6:7-8 encourages us that, "With good will render service, as to the Lord, and not to men, knowing that whatever good things each one does, this he will receive back from the Lord, whether slave or free."

A person wrote, "I remember working at a county-funded job where many employees sat idle due to an excess of positions. It was tempting to join their slothfulness. However, by consciously reminding myself that I was working for the Lord, I was able to remain diligent. As a result, when I was offered a better job, no one was surprised."

The Witness of Patience and Hard Work

In the secular world, success is often attributed to persistent effort and dedication. Most people scoff at get-rich-quick schemes, understanding that real achievement requires consistent hard work and perseverance. Proverbs reinforces this truth, and Galatians 6:9 reminds us not to become weary in doing good, as we will reap a harvest in due time if we do not give up. Working steadily builds character and earns respect even when results aren't immediate. It reflects Christ's character and honors God, attracting others to Him.

This is why Paul instructs believers in 1 Thessalonians 4:11-12 to work diligently and live in a way that wins the respect of outsiders. Persistent hard work aligns with biblical principles of patience and perseverance.

When unbelievers display more patience and dedication in pursuing their goals than Christians, it raises questions. What message are we sending when we, as believers, become impatient and quit prematurely on worthy projects? If a Christian who lacks persistence and discipline at work hands their unbelieving boss a tract about Jesus or shares about their faith at a company-wide meeting, do you think they hold much credibility?

How we present ourselves professionally directly affects our credibility when sharing spiritual messages. A message from someone undisciplined and lazy often lacks impact and can suggest a sense of entitlement rather than demonstrating the transformation that comes from a life lived for God. Hard work and perseverance are powerful witnesses to unbelievers. When Christians embody these traits, they reflect the character of Christ, who calls us to be steadfast in all areas of life.

A Cautionary Tale of Dishonesty and Laziness

I once knew a man who professed to be a Christian but exploited others for his gain. He launched a business venture, convincing countless investors to give him money. A close friend of mine in ministry, who had little money, invested $40,000 of his retirement, only to lose it all. This man spent the investors' money on leisure, never putting in a day's work to advance the project.

When I met him, he requested a list of wealthy people I knew so he could persuade them to invest in his venture. Recognizing his dishonesty, I refused. The next day, I received one of the most abusive and vile letters I have ever encountered. He said he never wanted to see me again.

Proverbs 30:15 (MSG) says, "A leech has twin daughters named 'Gimme' and 'Gimme more.'" This is the mindset of those who pursue instant gratification at the expense of integrity.

Though he claimed to follow Christ, this man led no one to Him. His laziness, fraud, and lack of discipline ruined his reputation and tarnished the name of Christ. To make matters worse, when the authorities caught up with him, he manipulated his wife into taking the blame, and she went to prison instead of him. This man's story is a stark warning about the dangers of seeking shortcuts and living without integrity.

Contrast this with the many unbelievers who work hard, knowing that "Rome wasn't built in a day." These individuals understand the value of patience and dedication, while some Christians, like this man, resort to schemes and shortcuts to get as much as they can as quickly as possible. Proverbs 30:15 (MSG) says, "A leech has twin daughters named 'Gimme' and 'Gimme more.'" This is the mindset of those who pursue instant gratification at the expense of integrity.

The Christian Call to Hard Work and Patience

As believers, we must embrace hard work, patience, and persistence. We should never be ashamed of honest labor's slow, steady process, even if it doesn't lead to immediate success or wealth. It's not about quick riches but about honoring God through our dedication and discipline. As Proverbs 13:11 reminds us, "Dishonest money dwindles, but whoever gathers money little by little makes it grow."

While we may not achieve overnight riches, we uphold the name of Christ by our diligence and earn the respect of both believers and unbelievers. At the end of our lives, it will be said of us that we lived with integrity, worked hard, and honored God in everything we did. People will weep at our funerals, and perhaps some will come to Christ because they saw in us a faithful, disciplined life.

Practical Applications for Persistent Self-Discipline

Commit to Long-Term Effort: Success, whether in faith, career, or personal growth, is achieved over time. Commit to the long game, knowing that rewards come in due time. Someone once commented, "I've always been shy, especially about sharing my faith. For years, I avoided speaking up, afraid of rejection. But I felt convicted to start small—just talking to one person each day about God. At first, it was awkward and uncomfortable, and I faced a lot of resistance. But over time, I found my voice and confidence. Now, I lead a small group and have seen several people come to Christ. It's taken years, but God showed me that even the smallest steps of obedience can lead to great things."

Work with Integrity: Proverbs 12:11 says, "Those who work their land will have abundant food, but those who chase fantasies have no sense." Avoid shortcuts or schemes that promise quick success. Honest, steady work is what ultimately leads to respect and prosperity. A person expressed, "I worked in a high-paying corporate job, but I constantly felt pressured to engage in unethical practices to boost profits. It tore at my conscience, and I knew I couldn't stay. I took a leap of faith and left, even though it meant a huge pay cut. I started my own business and committed to ethical practices. It's been a slow climb, but the peace I have is worth more than any paycheck. God has blessed my efforts, and I now have clients who respect and trust me because they know I won't compromise my integrity."

Be a Witness Through Your Work: As Paul instructed in 1 Thessalonians 4:11-12, let your work and discipline win the respect of outsiders. Your hard work can be a powerful witness to those around you. Live in such a way that your efforts draw others toward the truth of Christ. A person in the business world told me, "I work in a corporate office where faith isn't a topic of discussion. But I've made it my mission to show Christ through my work ethic and integrity. One day, a colleague approached me and said, 'I've noticed how you handle pressure and treat everyone respectfully. What's your secret?' It opened the door for me to share my faith and the peace I find in Christ. She began attending church with me, and eventually, she gave her life to Christ. I realized that sometimes, the most powerful witness isn't what we say but how we live."

Embrace the Process: Embrace the slow and steady process of building something meaningful—whether it's a career, a ministry, or personal growth in Christ. Proverbs 21:5 says, "The plans of the diligent lead to profit as surely as haste leads to poverty." A missionary said, "When I felt called to mission work in a foreign country, I knew I had to learn the language. It was a slow, frustrating process. There were days I wanted to give up, thinking

I'd never be fluent enough to truly connect with people. But I kept at it, studying and practicing every day. It took years, but eventually, I was able to share the Gospel in their language. The first time I led someone to Christ in their native tongue, I realized that every difficult step of the process had been worth it. God taught me that true impact requires dedication and patience."

Grace and Encouragement

When believers quit too soon, fall into laziness, or fail to live with self-discipline, it damages our witness. Never be ashamed of hard work. A life of steady dedication stands out in a world that often seeks instant gratification. If you are currently facing challenges or are tempted to give up, remember that God honors persistence. Don't become weary in doing good, for in due time, you will reap a harvest if you do not give up (Galatians 6:9). This doesn't mean we forever stay in a situation since the Lord does direct our steps into new ventures. However, my counsel has always been to do so at natural transitional moments, don't just up and quit. I liken it to my advice to a high school student wishing to quit the soccer team. "Finish the season first, then decide about next season."

For those of us who have struggled with discipline or feel like we've failed in this area, remember that it's never too late to start again. God's grace is abundant, and He can help you grow in discipline and perseverance. Philippians 4:13 reminds us, "I can do all this through him who gives me strength."

If you've been tempted to take shortcuts or give up too soon, ask God for the strength to persevere. The rewards may not come immediately, but you will see the fruit of your efforts in God's time. Trust that the Lord sees your hard work and that, in due time, He will bring a harvest.

EIGHT

Adaptability
(Bend but Do Not Break)

Life is unpredictable and full of challenges that can test our resolve and shake our foundations. In these moments, adapting and responding with faith and resilience becomes crucial. Adaptability isn't just about surviving difficult times; it's about thriving in them, finding new ways to grow, and "going with the flow," showing those around us the strength that comes from trusting God through every storm.

It may be easy to confuse adaptability with resilience. They are similar, as both require us to reevaluate and adjust to failure, a change in plans, or failed expectations. However, resilience is the ability to stand up after we've been knocked down—to bounce back stronger than ever and recover from setbacks. Adaptability is moving with changes as they come, like a tree that bends in the wind but doesn't break. Whether it's a sudden job loss, a heartbreaking loss, or a daunting change in circumstances, the people we care about need us to be steady and strong—not rigid, but flexible, adjusting to life's twists without losing hope or purpose, changing strategies and approaches as needed.

When we remain steadfast in our faith, we demonstrate God's grace in action, inspiring those around us to see that true strength is found not in never falling but in rising again, trusting that God is at work in every step we take. In years such as an election year, we may find ourselves in a new political setting—one we voted for or didn't. In either case, many will watch our reactions: do we wickedly fight the situation or adapt with a new, holy determination?

Christians must model this, rising after setbacks with faith and perseverance. When adversity strikes, the world expects adaptability. But apart from an observing world, God calls us to be this kind of person who trusts that all things work together for the good of those who love God and are called according to His purpose (Romans 8:28).

Consider the following testimonies of those who have adapted in the face of life going differently than planned. Instead of breaking, they show us how to bend, experiencing more of God's grace and blessing.

Single Mother After Divorce: "When my husband left, I felt like everything was falling apart. But I knew I couldn't collapse for my kids' sake. I leaned on my faith, trusted God's plan, and found strength I didn't know I had. I went back to school, got a job, and built a new life for us. Now, when my children look at me, they see a mother who stood strong in her faith and found hope in the hardest times."

Teacher During COVID-19: "When the pandemic turned everything upside down, I was overwhelmed. I went from a lively classroom to struggling with remote learning. I felt lost but knew I couldn't let my students down. I asked God for strength and adapted by learning new technology and finding creative ways to connect. It was tough, but my students and I made it through together because we didn't give up."

Athlete Facing Career-Ending Injury: "I was at the top of my game when an injury took me out. It felt like my dreams were over. But instead of giving up, I prayed and asked God for guidance. I shifted my focus to coaching and mentoring young athletes, using my experience to help others. It wasn't the future I envisioned, but it's become more fulfilling than I ever imagined. God truly opened new doors when one closed."

Veteran Adjusting to Civilian Life: "Returning from combat was harder than I expected. I felt out of place, lost, and angry. But I knew I couldn't let those feelings control me. I leaned on my faith, sought therapy, joined a support group, and found a new purpose in helping other vets. God gave me the strength to move forward, and now I'm using my experiences to make a difference."

Adoptive Parent Adjusting to New Realities: "Adopting an older child came with challenges I wasn't prepared for—behavioral issues, trauma, distrust. I had to change my expectations and learn new parenting skills, all while trusting God to guide us. It wasn't easy, but I held onto my faith and didn't give up. Now, we've built a loving family, growing together in trust and love."

Immigrant Starting Over in a New Country: "Moving to a new country with nothing but hope was terrifying. Language barriers, financial struggles, cultural differences—it felt like everything was against me. But I trusted God to lead the way. I took night classes, found a job, and slowly built a life here. It wasn't easy, but my faith kept me going. Now, I see how every challenge prepared me for a future I never imagined."

Pastor Leading Through Church Division: "Our church faced a division that almost tore us apart. Friends turned against me, and I was heartbroken. It would have been easier to leave, but I prayed for wisdom and trusted God's guidance. I stayed, listened, and worked to heal the rift. Today, our church is stronger and more united than ever. God turned a painful season into a testimony of His grace and faithfulness."

What the Scripture Says on Adaptability

- **2 Corinthians 4:8-9:** "We've been surrounded and battered by troubles, but we're not demoralized; we're not sure what to do, but we know that God knows what to do; we've been spiritually terrorized, but God hasn't left our side; we've been thrown down, but we haven't broken."

- **Matthew 7:24-25 (NIV):** "Therefore everyone who hears these words of mine and puts them into practice is like a wise man who built his house on the rock. The rain came down, the streams rose, and the winds blew and beat against that house, yet it did not fall because it had its foundation on the rock."

Paul highlights the paradox of Christian endurance. Though faced with extreme challenges—persecution, confusion, and oppression—the believer does not break because of God's sustaining presence. It conveys that while we may bend under the weight of trials, we are not destroyed, illustrating the profound spiritual adaptability required to remain firm in faith amidst adversity.

Though the Christ-follower has unanswered questions as to why the adversity came to them in the first place, as Sarah's mother said when diagnosed with cancer that took her life several weeks later, "I am not asking, 'Why me' but 'Why not me?'"

Both 2 Corinthians 4:8-9 and Matthew 7:24-25 inspire believers to trust God during difficult times. They remind us that while we may face overwhelming challenges, our spiritual foundation and reliance on God empower us to bend without breaking. This strength becomes a testimony to others, demonstrating the transformative power of faith. Jesus' parable emphasizes the importance of a solid spiritual foundation. A life built on His teachings can withstand life's storms, representing the ultimate adaptability—adjusting and responding to life's challenges without collapsing. This verse encourages believers to be rooted in Christ's wisdom, ensuring they remain unshaken and unbroken even when tested.

Most of us have heard of Dave Ramsey, Joni Eareckson Tada, and Corrie ten Boom. Each exemplified Christ-like adaptability uniquely, demonstrating that they bent but never broke.

Dave Ramsey: Faced with financial ruin early in his career, Dave Ramsey adapted by turning his personal financial crisis into a successful business and, later, a platform to teach others. He developed the "Financial Peace University" and authored books to guide people out of debt, using his experiences to shape his approach. Though broke, he did not break.

Joni Eareckson Tada: After a diving accident left her a quadriplegic, Joni adapted by becoming a powerful advocate for people with disabilities, founding Joni and Friends, a ministry dedicated to the support and inclusion of those with disabilities. She adapted by channeling her suffering into service and advocacy.

Corrie ten Boom: During World War II, Corrie ten Boom and her family hid Jews from the Nazis, leading to their arrest. Even in the concentration camp, Corrie maintained her faith and used her experiences to help others, sharing the message of forgiveness and Christ's love after the war. Her adaptability in such extreme circumstances, holding fast to her faith and offering hope to others, demonstrates that we need not snap in the face of evil.

When Adaptability Seems Impossible

When Christians crumble under adversity, it raises questions about the strength we claim to have in Christ. It's a sobering reality that even Spirit-filled believers can doubt God's love and turn away in disobedience. This life has troubles; some appear too large to overcome, much less adapt to. One person shared with me:

> "I prayed that God would change my circumstances. But when I didn't see an answer to my prayers, I stopped praying altogether. Looking back, I realize how easily a believer can become the person you described—questioning God's love and turning away. I was that person, and that decision to turn away from God led to the most painful years of my life. I had no positive impact on the unbelievers around me and now have deep sorrow over wasting those years."

Such stories are not uncommon. During World War II, my former Pastor of Visitation, Ainsley Barnwell, witnessed first-hand the devastation that shattered many people's faith. In

England, amidst the horrors of the Blitz, he pulled lifeless bodies from the rubble of bombed homes—innocent children among them. He saw something break in the hearts of many churchgoers. Overwhelmed by relentless trauma and loss, they turned away from God, their faith destroyed by the darkness around them.

Similarly, one night while out to eat after a Love and Respect Marriage Conference, the hostess shared her own crisis of faith. After her daughter lost her newborn, she felt utterly betrayed by God. "I had a little copper box filled with God's promises," she said, "but when my grandchild died, I felt abandoned. It was as though God hadn't kept His promise." I asked her if all the promises in her box were positive ones or if she included verses like "all who live godly in Christ Jesus will be persecuted" (2 Timothy 3:12). She admitted that they were all positive. Her story reminds us that when our understanding of God's promises is incomplete, we can feel deeply disillusioned when suffering comes.

I do not intend to minimize the overwhelming pain these individuals experienced. A person once wrote to me, "Watching my mother battle depression and feeling utterly abandoned by God, I couldn't reconcile her pain with a loving God. I pulled away from faith, doubting if He truly cared or even existed."

Years ago, a man who was carrying a heavy burden visited our church. As a pastor, he and his wife had endured the unimaginable loss of their four-year-old daughter. Such heartbreak shakes the very foundations of faith. In their suffering, a piercing question arose in their souls: Is God good? They never received an answer to why their daughter died, but this question became a lifeline, guiding them through the darkest valley of their lives. In the end, they chose to believe that God is good. However, in their congregation, several couples who had fervently prayed for the child's healing were crushed by the loss. Unable to reconcile why an all-loving and all-powerful God didn't heal this innocent child, they left the church, turning their backs on God.

In times of "present distress," as Paul references in 1 Corinthians 7, some husbands and wives turn completely away from the Lord, convinced that if something so terrible could happen, God must not have been there or is even against them. They lose heart—the very thing Jesus urged us not to do (Luke 18:1). Instead of viewing hardships and unanswered questions as opportunities to deepen their love for Christ and for each other, they follow the path of least resistance, drifting toward the ways of the world. Some seek solace in worldly pleasures rather than in pleasing God and each other.

Tragically, when they have children, their disillusionment can cause these little ones to stumble in their faith, something Jesus sternly warned against: "It would be better for them to have a millstone hung around their neck and be drowned in the depths of the sea" (Matthew 18:6). The tragedy extends beyond their own loss of spiritual grounding to the seeds of doubt and disillusionment they plant in the hearts of their children.

This mindset can be deeply rooted in hubris and arrogance—believing oneself so important that God owes protection from unjust suffering. And if He does not prevent it, we feel justified in denouncing or denying Him.

Practical Applications for Adaptability

In this life, there will be troubles (John 16:33). When we face those times, we have the choice: to adapt or to succumb to our circumstances. As Christians, we are not immune to trials, trauma, or loss. Whether it's something as large as a personal loss or as temporary as a change in political leadership, both believers and non-believers alike are watching to see how we come to terms with life turning out differently than we thought. How can we apply adaptability in our daily lives in a way that honors God and points others to him? Adaptability doesn't mean pretending that hardships aren't real or difficult. If you are facing adversity, take heart. God can use your trials to strengthen you and to be a testimony to those around you. Keep rising, keep bending without breaking, and trust that God will work through your adaptability for His glory.

See Things as an Opportunity to Trust God in the Face of Unanswered Questions: In times of confusion and uncertainty, it's essential to consciously decide whether to trust God's sovereignty or be overwhelmed by doubt. Recognizing that not all questions will have immediate answers requires a leap of faith, trusting that God's plan is good, even when we can't see it clearly. This mindset shapes our response to the unknown. Even Jesus faced an unanswered question on the cross when He cried, "My God, my God, why have you forsaken me?" (Matthew 27:46). I challenge myself with this question: Will I trust God in the face of what I don't understand in light of what I do understand about Jesus in the Gospels? Or, will I distrust (and denounce) God in the face of what I don't understand, even in the face of what I do understand about Jesus in the Gospels?

Look for the Stepping Stones Forward When Feeling Flooded with Difficulties: When life's challenges seem insurmountable, it's easy to feel overwhelmed and paralyzed. Choosing to search for small, actionable steps forward actively—no matter how insignificant they may seem—keeps us moving. Though seemingly small, these stepping stones help us maintain momentum, trusting that God will guide us through one step at a time.

Be a Beacon of Light to Others Experiencing a Similar Darkness: In our struggles, we can shine God's light on others facing similar trials. By sharing our faith journey, we can offer hope and encouragement, showing that God's presence can be felt even in darkness. It's about letting our hardships become a testimony of His sustaining grace.

Foster an Unbreakable Spirit: Adaptability doesn't mean ignoring pain but embracing a mindset that refuses to be defeated. It's a commitment to stand firm in faith despite setbacks and to view each challenge as a chance to grow stronger, even if in a different way than planned. An unbreakable spirit is forged in the fire of adversity, becoming a powerful witness of God's strength in our weakness.

Pray and Anticipate that God Is Working All Things Together for Good: Prayer is more than just a request for help; it's an act of surrender and expectation. When we pray with anticipation, we express confidence that God is at work, even in the most difficult circumstances. This mindset shifts our focus from what's wrong to what God can do, filling us with peace and hope as we await His timing and purpose to unfold.

These applications help you live out the principle of "bending without breaking," showing that true adaptability is rooted in a deep trust in God's purpose and provision, even when life feels out of control.

NINE

Communication Skills
(It's Not What You Say, It's How You Say It)

Effective communication is not just about the message but the delivery. How we communicate is just as important as what we communicate. Scripture emphasizes speaking with gentleness and respect, which defuses conflict and reflects Christ's love. Whether discussing sensitive topics like politics, issues in marriage, or our boss at work, how we speak can make or break relationships.

Scripture emphasizes the power of gentle, loving speech. Proverbs 15:1 states, "A gentle answer turns away wrath, but a harsh word stirs up anger." In my book *Speak Your Mind*, I help readers dissect the type of communicator they are and give simple tools to help filter what should and should not be said. This results in you, as the communicator, being "heard" much more effectively. One simple rule that can be hard to follow is speaking truth with love (Ephesians 4:15). But when we do, it allows us to stand firm on convictions without alienating others. Whether in marriage, ministry, or work, how we deliver our message determines whether people will be open to it.

Communicating clearly, empathically, and carefully makes all the difference in maintaining peace and understanding. Even in stressful situations, those we care about need us to communicate well. And, to Jesus, how we speak lovingly to those who deem us their enemies also matters.

The Common Attitude Among Some

"I could not care less about how I sound. People need to deal with the truth."

This mindset often justifies harsh or abrasive speech, but being "right" doesn't excuse being unkind. My wife Sarah often reminds those attending our marriage conference, "You can be right but wrong at the top of your voice." Our tone and approach must match the spirit of the message we wish to convey.

Truth need not be delivered with hostility and contempt to ensure the message gets through. It has the opposite effect. Such hostility and contempt are the default modes used by some individuals who do not believe truth carries its weight and demonstrate that they are out of control emotionally. This behavior can create a destructive relationship pattern, making it difficult for the other person to respond with love or respect and much less likely to hear the message of the communicator, even if it is true. A cycle of negativity ensues where each reacts to the other's reaction. Hostility and contempt trigger hostility and contempt, escalating to a level where both consider the other an enemy.

A husband shared, "One of the largest issues right now in my marriage is my tone with my wife. I often don't realize that I even have a tone, and when I do recognize that I have a tone, I notice that it's hard for me to stop my frustrated tone. Any advice for being more self-aware in the moment and how to transition to a more loving tone, even in moments of frustration?"

I have also heard this: "Years ago, I acknowledged that 'tone' was crucial in communication. Since then, I've worked hard to change my approach: softening my voice, adding humor, slowing down, 'softening my eyes,' asking questions before making accusations, and using more respectful language like 'Sir' and 'Ma'am,' along with plenty of "Please," "Pardon," and "Thank You." In recent years, I've become more aware of how other people's tone affects me. But the question remains: HOW DO WE CHANGE OUR TONE, while still maintaining influence and commanding respect—without being marginalized, minimized, or coming across as fake, phony, or 'syrupy sweet'? How do we stay true to ourselves and our culture?"

We can agree that this person truly "gets it" and is doing an outstanding job. They've adjusted their tone, and while they still wonder if this approach will continue to command respect and maintain influence, I assure them it will! It's such a simple change it can be hard to understand the magnitude of its results. Yes, there will always be those resistant, even to Jesus Himself, but generally speaking, a respectful tone profoundly impacts people's hearts.

In addition, something that helps me is being "the first" to act. Here are six things I try to do before the other person speaks, which often motivates the other person to follow suit.

My Checklist of "Firsts" for Better Communication

1. Ask First: *I need to remind myself to ask questions first to clarify the other person's perspective before blurting out what I think they are saying.*

2. Understand First: *I need to remind myself to seek to understand first what the other person is saying or not saying before demanding they understand me.*

3. Paraphrase Back First: *I need to remind myself to paraphrase what the other person has said to confirm understanding before adding my perspective, ensuring they feel heard. I will ask, "Do I understand you correctly?"*

4. Acknowledge Feelings First: *I need to remind myself to acknowledge their feelings first by recognizing the emotions of the other person, such as saying, "I can see this is really important to you," to show empathy and respect. I may not agree since they could be wrong for feeling as they do, but it is best to acknowledge their feelings in the beginning. This allows them to feel heard and seen. However, just because I say, "I can see that you are upset," does not mean I think they have a right to be upset.*

5. Validate Facts First: *I need to remind myself to validate their facts first by saying something like, "I can see why you would feel that way," before expressing my own views. Often, people do have valid reasons for feeling as they do based on what happened, and frankly, I often feel the same way. Who is to say whose feelings are valid and whose are not? Though they may have limited facts or one-sided viewpoints, validating what they do know validates them as people and allows them to see how there might be more to the story.*

6. Check My Assumptions First: *I need to remind myself to check my assumptions first by asking, "Can you tell me more about what you mean by that?" to ensure I'm not misinterpreting their words or intentions. This is a repeat of the above, but I am biased, and I mishear. My mind quickly tabulates, and when I feel insecure or attacked, I can read into a situation that isn't there. When I don't practice these steps, I increase the odds that not only will what I say be incorrect, but I will make my incorrect assertions loudly and disrespectfully, potentially negatively affecting the course of the conversation.*

How Do We Talk?

Interestingly, the secular world values effective communication skills, advocating for civility and respectful discourse. Though people may not always live up to these standards, they still expect their opponents, colleagues, family, or neighbors to communicate without hate and disdain. For Christians, how we speak is crucial not only to maintain common decency in discourse but also to maintain common decency in the home.

When I was a senior pastor, a person in my congregation felt troubled by what the spiritual leadership at our church preferred to do related to the church's vision and possible relocation. He talked divisively and angrily, though there was no compromise of Scripture in the proposal. It was okay that he could not support the choices being made about building a new facility, but his lack of gentleness stirred up the emotions of a handful of people to also turn against the board of elders. At one point in his life, he felt justified in feeling the leadership was sinfully wrong in their decisions and saying so. "You are not following God's will on this," he confidently spoke. But the Lord spoke to his conscience, asking him, "Are those leaders violating My Word and Will or seeking to do it? And can you knowingly say their motives are impure, or are you speculating and presuming?" He discovered that the Lord was revealing to him that he had a right to disagree but not to show contempt toward the leaders simply because their methods and strategies differed from his. He realized this was a gray area or preference issue. Once he recognized this, he softened and made his opinion known without judging the board as sinfully wrong.

In parenting, teenagers express their anger in disrespectful ways. This distresses every mother and father. We don't deserve to be dishonored; they must be confronted and corrected. I have coached such parents to tell a teen boy, for example, "You are becoming an honorable young man, and I expected you to tell us what you feel you need to say, but do so with a respectful tone reflecting the honorable man you are becoming. As I am seeking to speak gently and respectfully to you, may I invite you to begin again and share what you feel but to do so with a respectful tone?" Typically, our gentle answer will defuse the teen's anger.

People in our neighborhood may know we are Christ-followers. Watching us interface with our teen son like this creates a positive and lasting impression. We aren't doing this to be impressive, but it is part of a kingdom mindset to allow our parenting to be a factor in winning hearts, influencing lives, and appealing to the world along the lines of virtues they value. A parent in the neighborhood may eventually turn to us to ask for help with their teen. Eventually, our friendship with them may deepen, and perhaps one day, we may be able to introduce them to Christ.

What the Scripture Says on Speaking

The Bible offers clear guidance on the importance of communicating with grace and gentleness:

- **James 1:19:** "Everyone should be quick to listen, slow to speak, and slow to become angry."

- **Ephesians 4:29:** "Do not let any unwholesome talk come out of your mouths, but only what is helpful for building others up according to their needs, that it may benefit those who listen."

- **Colossians 4:6:** "Let your speech always be with grace, as though seasoned with salt, so that you will know how you should respond to each person."

The same applies to the married.

- **Colossians 3:19:** "Husbands, do not be harsh with your wives."

- **Proverbs 27:15:** "A continual dripping on a rainy day and a quarrelsome wife are alike."

A couple once wrote me, "It took years of saying things at the wrong time, in the wrong way, and then being mad and frustrated with each other before we finally realized that it's not only what you say that is important, but when you say it, how you say it, and if you should say it."

"The Crazy Cycle," a term I use in my book *Love & Respect*, has begun. She feels unloved and responds disrespectfully. He, in turn, feels disrespected and reacts in anger, which she perceives as even more unloving. Each desire is not wrong, but both react poorly when emotions and hurt take over. If it's a summer evening with the windows open, or if their unbelieving friend is in the kitchen getting a drink, their raised voices become an unfortunate testimony to those around them.

We must remember that marriage symbolizes Christ and the church (Ephesians 5:32). If non-believers witness Christian couples speaking harshly to each other, it distorts the image of God's love. Our marriages should reflect unity and grace, drawing others toward Christ, not pushing them away. Paul's words in Romans 2:21-24 remind us that hypocrisy leads others to blaspheme God. Our words and how we say them must align with our faith to maintain integrity and witness.

The Impact of Communication During Political Seasons

Maintaining Grace Under Pressure: It's easy to let passion overshadow kindness during political debates or discussions. Issues like abortion, climate change, or freedom of speech and religion stir intense emotions. While we should never compromise our convictions, it's essential to communicate them with gentleness and respect. Again, the truth will carry its own weight. A harsh or insulting tone will only convince our opponent that our words are more mean than meaningful.

Historical Example: Very early Christians opposed infanticide, and yet, in those times, unwanted infants were left "expositi"—

which is Latin for "exposed ones"—or left neglected to the elements.[5] However, there is no report of violent protests. The believers took the abandoned children into their homes, and their loving actions and gentle words transformed the Roman world's view of Christianity, illustrating that our communication and conduct should reflect Christ's love, even on matters like infanticide. I surface this issue of infanticide to demonstrate that we must take a stand and act in alignment with our biblical conflicts. Political and social issues that break our hearts cannot be ignored, and we must do more than communicate with words but take constructive Christ-like action. This is what will win hearts, not heated keyboard debates.

Practical Applications for Communication Skills

While we may share something "right" or "true," our words will fall on deaf ears if not spoken with gentleness, respect, and love. The practical applications below show how a different, scripture-based approach can transform our everyday interactions.

Speak with Gentleness: Proverbs 15:1 reminds us that a gentle answer can de-escalate conflicts and build bridges, even in disagreements. A person reported, "I realized that when I communicated my frustrations harshly, it shut down conversations. Now I speak more gently, [and others are] more open and responsive."

Watch Your Tone: Colossians 3:19 advises against harshness, which often causes defensiveness and strife. A respectful tone fosters understanding. Someone once commented, "I knew my words were right, but something felt off. My harsh tone was creating walls instead of building bridges. I began consciously softening my voice, and it was like a switch flipped. My spouse and kids responded with openness instead of defensiveness."

Seek to Understand First: James 1:19 encourages us to be "quick to listen, slow to speak, and slow to anger." Listening shows respect, helps avoid rash responses, and can help bridge connections, even amidst disagreement. A daughter said, "I used to argue with my mom all the time about politics. Then I decided to really listen to why she believed what she did. I didn't agree with everything, but I began to understand her fears and experiences. It brought us closer."

Choose Words Wisely: Ephesians 4:29 instructs us to speak words that build others up and avoid harmful speech. At our Love and Respect Conference, I urge those in attendance to ask themselves this question before speaking: "Is that which I am about to say going to sound loving and respectful?" Someone told me, "I started using respectful words instead of reacting angrily, and it made a huge difference."

Practice What You Preach: When practicing what we preach, Jesus reminds us in Matthew 7:3-5 to address the "plank in our own eye" before pointing out the faults in others. So, if we're calling for a cleaner environment, we must first take responsibility for our own spaces and actions. For instance, I love what I once heard. An adult told some young people, "If you demand that we clean up the environment, start by cleaning up your own room!" Our actions speak louder than words. When we take steps to model what we're asking for, it builds our credibility and makes it easier for others to take our message seriously.

While the world values communication skills for success, Christians are called to go further. Our words should not just meet, but exceed expectations, reflecting Christ's humility, love, and grace (Ephesians 4:2). Our distinct way of communicating can, therefore, draw others to Christ.

Building Trust Through Truthful But Humble Communication

A man wrote to me, saying, "I was quick to judge and speak harshly at work, but after realizing the impact of my words, I started responding more patiently and understandingly. One day, a colleague confronted me angrily, and instead of snapping back, I took a deep breath and said, 'I'm sorry you feel that way. Can we talk about it?' This simple question, humbly asked, changed the entire conversation, and we were able to resolve the issue calmly."

A police officer shared how changing his communication style helped de-escalate a potentially dangerous situation. Instead of issuing commands aggressively, he spoke calmly and respectfully to a distressed individual. The person, who had been agitated and confrontational, gradually calmed down and complied. The officer's compassionate tone prevented violence and led to a peaceful resolution.

Sarah, my wife, loves this approach: humbly and honestly ask the other person, "How did you come to that conclusion on that issue?" Humbly asking this question shifts the focus from confrontation to understanding. This approach helps us avoid immediately telling someone they are wrong or asserting our own rightness. It creates a space for dialogue and shows respect for the other person's viewpoint. By exploring what is underneath their choices, we can better understand their perspective, reduce defensiveness, and build a foundation for meaningful and respectful conversation.

For me, a pivotal moment came in college. The question asked by a professor in a class on Interpersonal Dynamics during my sophomore year—"Is that which I am about to say going to build trust or undermine trust?"—revolutionized my thinking. This question ignited a desire to discover more about effective communication and helped me communicate in ways that sounded loving and respectful. That question prepared me to speak in an inviting, not provocative tone. That was important to me since, during that summer, the Chaplain asked me to speak in my college chapel at Wheaton College. Afterward, I went to him for feedback, hoping he'd tell me I am the next Billy Graham or affirming that I would be a great pastor and shepherd of a local church. Instead, he looked at me and said, "I have one piece of advice. Don't beat the sheep."

None of us are perfect communicators, but God's grace is sufficient. Take heart and trust that we all can grow and begin again through prayer, humility, and guidance from the Holy Spirit. Even in my seventies, after studying God's word for years and years, I have to ask myself: will my words reflect Christ or create unnecessary conflict?

TEN

Authenticity
(Honesty Is the Best Policy)

Most decent humans, regardless of their faith, value honesty and fairness and have some type of personal ethics. Most people respond positively and like those they believe to be genuine and humble. By being truthful about ourselves and speaking the truth—the whole truth—consistently, we build a solid reputation with others over time. This integrity serves us well and draws others towards the things of Christ.

Honesty is the Best Policy

Years ago, I noticed how often people say, "Honest to God" during conversations. Not only are they invoking God's name, but they are also doing so in all likelihood to cover up a lie.

I recall being part of a conversation where one person said, "I'll be honest with you." My friend responded, "Well, what have you been with me up to this point?" I thought, "Wow, what an insightful observation! Why say it when honesty should be the default?" Since then, I've shared that perspective numerous times when people say, "I'll be honest with you." They cease using that sentence immediately, and, in the case of some, I know it is due to their less-than-honest exchanges up to that point.

Whether in business, politics, or personal relationships, honesty is universally valued—because no one wants to be lied to or treated unethically. Even though people may often fall short of these ideals, an overarching belief remains that integrity matters. This shared understanding exists because it's morally right and creates trust, essential for functioning relationships and society. If you know someone who was historically dishonest with you, you slowly begin to distrust them, keeping them at a distance because of their lack of integrity.

Yes, people are less than honest because lying often works. People wouldn't lie if they knew they'd be found out 100% of the time. Lying usually happens because we believe it can work to our advantage, advancing our agenda or needs. However, the believer must square off with the reality that God sees all and values truth. While lying might offer short-term gains, it ultimately distances us from God's delight and damages our witness. Our allegiance is not to what works in this world but to what is right in God's eyes. In all conversations, a thinking believer knows they just have an audience of one (Hebrews 4:13).

Furthermore, lying is hard work. We must remember the truth and the lie and not forget the lie we told. If someone catches us in the lie, we now have to lie about the lie or risk humiliating ourselves by admitting the truth. We have to lie to stay ahead of other lies we have told because lies beget lies. Honesty is the best policy because lying is an exhausting cycle. Scripture reminds us: "Whoever walks in integrity walks securely" (Proverbs 10:9).

Why Integrity Matters to the World

Even though we often see politicians, businesses, or individuals bending the truth, the expectation of integrity remains. People may lie, but they still expect others to be truthful. This double standard can be frustrating, but it reveals a deeper truth: everyone wants to be treated honestly and fairly. When promises are broken or unethical decisions are made, trust is shattered, and relationships are damaged.

Directly lying, altering the truth, or even lying by omission can severely affect those around us. Read some of the following testimonies to understand the importance of honesty as the best policy:

Business Leader: "After losing a major client due to a minor but deliberate omission, I learned that integrity in business isn't just about following rules; it's about building trust that, once broken, can rarely be restored."

Politician: "I realized that people may forgive mistakes, but they won't forget being deceived."

Friend: "I confided in someone I thought was a close friend, only to have my words twisted and used against me. It wasn't just betrayal—it shattered my ability to trust others with my heart. What they shared did reflect some of my exaggerated moments of venting, but I trusted my friend to keep those excesses private, never imagining they'd turn around and share what I had blurted out. They selectively used my over-the-top words against me in front of others, which I couldn't deny other than say I really didn't mean the semi-rant. It felt like a deliberate, mean-spirited attempt to discredit me."

CEO: "When I came forward about a financial misstep I made in our company, which I could have covered up, I feared backlash. Instead, I gained the respect of my team, who valued my transparency over my wrongdoing. I paid the price for that inexcusable action, but when I acted on 'honesty is the best policy' I eventually turned the corner and benefited. People are forgiving."

Employee: "I embellished my work on a project I hadn't contributed to. When I confessed my part honestly, it cost me a promotion, but my integrity remained intact, and that's something no title can replace. It cleared my conscience, which was eating away at me."

Volunteer: "I once saw a nonprofit leader misrepresent our efforts to donors. It was devastating to see a cause I believed in compromised by a lack of honesty."

Spouse: "After my husband confessed to hiding a financial issue, it was tough, but I respected him for being truthful. It was the first step in rebuilding our marriage and our trust."

Teacher: "When I admitted to my students that I didn't have all the answers, I saw firsthand that honesty doesn't diminish authority; it deepens it."

Church Member: "A church leader fell from grace due to hidden sins. It wasn't just his actions but the dishonest cover up that shook our faith community, teaching us that truth is the bedrock of any spiritual relationship."

Entrepreneur: "I lost investors by being upfront about the risks of my startup. I may have overstated the risks. But I've gained partners who trust me to always tell them the truth, even when it's hard."

HR Manager: "I discovered that my company's hiring practices were biased against minority candidates. When I brought it up to the executives, I was told to keep quiet or risk losing my job. I chose to speak out anyway and pushed for fair and equitable hiring policies. I never denounced hiring based on merit and competency, however minorities who were qualified were excluded from interviews. I faced hostility and isolation at work, but eventually, my persistence paid off. Not only did we change our hiring process, but I also gained the respect of my colleagues for standing up for what was right. Today, we have a more diverse and inclusive workplace, and I'm proud to have been part of that change."

High School Coach: "I caught one of our star athletes cheating on an exam. I knew reporting it would disqualify him from the upcoming championship game, and the pressure to stay silent was intense. But I couldn't compromise my values because I had identified myself as a Christian, and people knew I was on the board at my church. I reported the incident and faced backlash from parents and school officials. We lost the game, but the athlete learned a valuable lesson. Years later, he thanked me for holding him accountable and told me it changed his life."

The Impact of Christian Integrity

Our integrity is one of the greatest ways we can reflect Christ to the world. When believers fail to live up to their word or engage in dishonest behavior, it damages our testimony. Non-Christians may not always live by the same moral code, but they expect Christians to be different. This expectation is even higher for us because of our faith.

Consider this: Have you ever heard an unbeliever say, "I want what that lying Christian has"? Of course not. Even non-believers value truth and integrity and often point out when a Christian falls short in this area. Unbelievers expect us to uphold a higher standard, and lying provides them with a reason to dismiss the faith altogether, saying, "If this is how Christians act, why should I follow Christ?"

Our choices around integrity can either confirm or contradict the message of Christ. When we walk in truth, we reflect God's character. And it is through this reflection that others are drawn to Him. Said differently, Jesus said Satan is the father of lies, and when we give into conscious, willful falsehood, nothing good will come of this, and if it does, our relationship with the Lord suffers. On the other hand, when we stand with integrity, we glorify God, and others see our efforts.

Take this testimony from a non-profit director, for example: "We were struggling to meet our fundraising goals, and a wealthy donor offered a large contribution with strings attached—it required endorsing a political position that went against our mission. Rejecting the money meant missing vital funds, but compromising our values would have undermined everything we stood for. I turned down the donation and explained why to my team and our supporters. It was a difficult decision, but it rallied our community. Donations poured in from people who valued our integrity, and we exceeded our goal without compromising our principles."

While it may be easy to simply "not lie" in overtly harmful ways, I challenge you to look for ways to integrate integrity into your daily life. This is "living above the bar" —exceeding minimal expectations. When we let integrity and honesty direct our actions, even the small ones, it will be much easier to incorporate integrity and honesty in the "make it or break it" moments.

Practical Applications for Living with Integrity

While it may be easy to simply "not lie" in overtly harmful ways, I challenge you to look for ways to integrate integrity into your daily life. This is "living above the bar"—exceeding minimal expectations. When we let integrity and honesty direct our actions, even the small ones, it will be much easier to incorporate integrity and honesty in the "make it or break it" moments.

Keep Your Promises: One of the simplest ways to show integrity is to keep your word. Whether it's a promise to a friend, a commitment at work, or something as small as being on time, our actions should align with our words. An owner wrote, "I promised my employees I wouldn't lay them off during the recession. I took no salary, sold personal assets, and kept the company afloat. It was rough, but keeping my promise mattered more than comfort." James 5:12 reinforces this, saying, "Let your 'Yes' be yes, and your 'No' be no, so that you may not fall under condemnation."

Be Honest in Small Things: Integrity isn't just about the big moral decisions; it's about being honest in everyday situations. Luke 16:10 reminds us, "Whoever is faithful in very little is also faithful in much, and whoever is unrighteous in very little is also unrighteous in much." Small acts of dishonesty, like cutting corners or exaggerating the truth, erode our integrity over time. A story of a boy, excited that his bus ticket wasn't collected, told his father about his financial gain. However, instead of praising the son, his father said, "You sold your honor for the price of that ticket." This is a firm response but a poignant point reminding us that small choices impact and reveal our character.

Admit Mistakes: We all make mistakes; when we do, it's crucial to admit them. Humility is part of integrity and owning up rather than covering up, restores trust and reflects Christ's grace in our lives (Proverbs 28:13). In an episode of *Gunsmoke*, Matt Dillon admits his mistake after misjudging a man. His willingness to acknowledge his error, despite the guilt it caused, exemplifies the importance of owning up to one's mistakes to maintain integrity. The classic line he made after his friends sought to ease his pain, "Yeah, just a mistake, but it was my mistake and it was a bad one. I can't wish myself out of it with a few words".

Operate with Transparency: In business, ministry, or personal life, transparency breeds trust. Let your actions be open for others to see, and let your conduct be above reproach (2 Corinthians 8:21). In certain fields, there is a tendency never to admit wrongdoing to protect oneself. However, true integrity often requires the opposite approach. What do you think of this situation? "I was offered a substantial bribe, as a commissioner, to ignore a violation in a local construction project. The money could have changed my life, but it would have compromised my values and the safety of our community. I refused the money and reported the bribe attempt. The backlash was severe, and I faced criticism and threats. But standing firm in integrity showed others that I wasn't for sale. Though some think I am stupid, no one tries to bribe me. Today, I am known for being incorruptible, and people trust my leadership more than ever before and know that my faith in God is real. Several have come to my church when I invited them to our Easter services."

Practice What You Preach: As Christians, we must align our actions with the faith we profess. Romans 2:21-24 warns us about the dangers of hypocrisy: "You who teach others, do you not teach yourself? You who preach against stealing, do you steal?... God's name is blasphemed among the Gentiles because of you." Integrity means living consistently with what we say we believe. When asked by Carl F. Henry what was most important in life, Billy Graham immediately replied, "Integrity."

We might all feel like we aren't quite Billy Graham, but I'd encourage you to ask yourself and evaluate how you feel you are doing in the area of authenticity and honesty being the "best" policy. Do you believe it? Live it? Remember, your actions speak louder than your words, and while it can be easier to cut corners, it's a good filter to ask yourself, "Is what I'm about to do or say going to contradict or confirm the message of Christ?"

As we all try to be better witnesses to the world, let's quote Proverbs 28:13, "One who conceals his wrongdoings will not prosper, but one who confesses and abandons them will find compassion."

As you strive to live with integrity, trust that God will be abundantly compassionate toward you. Living authentically protects us from the damage dishonesty can cause, keeping our personal and financial resources focused on Christ's work. When we walk in integrity, we safeguard our witness and allow our lives to be a testament to the power and truth of the Gospel.

ELEVEN

Growth in Wellness
(You Are What You Eat)

Permit me to be upfront—we are talking about health, not beauty. Beauty is subjective and resides in the eye of the beholder, but the Bible also reminds us that "Charm is deceptive, and beauty is vain…" (Proverbs 31:30, ESV). The aim here is health, which is a biblical priority. The Bible speaks clearly about the importance of maintaining and nurturing our health. Note the Biblical references to health, and that is the focus here.

- **Proverbs 4:22 (ESV):** "health to the body."
- **Jeremiah 33:6 (ESV):** "Behold, I will bring to it health and healing…"
- **Proverbs 16:24 (ESV):** "health to the body."
- **Proverbs 3:7-8 (NIV):** "bring health to your body."

- **3 John 1:2 (NIV):** "Dear friend, I pray that you may enjoy good health and that all may go well with you, even as your soul is getting along well."

This emphasis on health, rather than external appearance, encourages us to prioritize wellness and well-being as part of our stewardship of the bodies God has given us.

As with most of the chapters in this book, I have had to face living above the bar, and that is the case on my growth in wellness. From third grade to eighth grade, I struggled with my weight. I wore Husky pants, and my legs rubbed together when I ran. My belly hung over the front of my pants, and sometimes people called me "fatty." I cried, feeling humiliated and isolated. To this day, I deeply empathize with those who struggle with their weight. Just recently, I chatted with a good friend who shared that she weighed 240 pounds in fifth grade and over 300 pounds in college. My heart broke for her as she described the pain and loneliness she felt.

Both of us recognized that our struggles with weight came from a greater source of pain. For us, our families of origin played a significant role in our struggles with weight gain. For me, the issue began in third grade when my parents got back together after five years of separation. From that year through eighth grade, I used food—so I think—as a way to cope with the emotional turmoil in our home. While my parents had gotten back together, they still didn't get along, and the stress took its toll on me.

I gained weight during those years, and it truly weighed me down—both physically and emotionally. Similarly, my friend described how the emotional pain she encountered as a child drove her to overeat, using food as a form of comfort. In her case, she was subjected to horrible abuse, which when her story is heard, people weep. I weep. Unfortunately, her coping mechanism only compounded the pain, creating a cycle that was difficult to break.

The good news is that we eventually reached a point where we said, "Enough" regardless of our environments. We knew that the loss of credibility, the poor self-image, and the health risks associated with being unhealthy outweighed any temporary relief that overeating provided. We realized that if we didn't take control of our health, we'd be losing far more than weight—losing our chance to live fully and serve others effectively. We knew people might accept us without addressing the issue, but we'd always feel like the "elephant in the room." That realization was a powerful motivator for change.

Caring for our health on all fronts enhances our ability to grow spiritually and emotionally. A healthy body, mind, and spirit allow us to serve God and others better. Our wellness contributes to sustained, long-term personal and spiritual growth. This chapter explores the deep connection between our physical well-being and overall growth, using personal stories and testimonies to illustrate the power of good stewardship of our bodies and the vital role Scripture plays in guiding us toward wellness.

What Is the Concern?

We are concerned that neglecting our physical health can significantly impact our bodies and spiritual and emotional well-being. The Bible tells us in 1 Corinthians 6:19-20 that our bodies are temples of the Holy Spirit and that we are called to honor God with them. This isn't about striving for perfection but recognizing that our choices profoundly impact our ability to live out our faith fully. It's about understanding that our health is not just a personal issue; it's a matter of stewardship, affecting our witness to others and our capacity to fulfill God's calling.

I've encountered some resistance when sharing my story. Someone once suggested that I shouldn't mention wearing "Husky" pants as it might offend or trigger others. But the truth is, I did wear Husky pants, and I can't erase my own story. As Ben Shapiro often says, "Facts don't care about your feelings." My purpose, however, isn't to be insensitive but to speak the truth in love. I deeply empathize with others who struggle, and my journey has made me passionate about wellness and health. However, we must address these matters compassionately while remembering that "honesty is the best policy." We encourage people to quit smoking, drinking, or gambling due to the harm they cause, but talking about eating habits and weight gain is increasingly becoming taboo. Mental health discussions are more accepted, but sidestepping the topic of physical well-being doesn't help anyone—it only leaves people trapped in unhealthy patterns.

I understand that factors like metabolism and medical conditions can influence the number we see on the scale, and that's not what I'm addressing here. I am equally burdened that some socio-economic groups can afford mostly processed foods that are often unhealthy and lacking in nutritional value. This makes it even more challenging for people in these communities to make healthy choices, as fresh, whole foods are either too expensive or inaccessible. While acknowledging these realities, my focus is on the habits we can change—being mindful of how we steward the bodies God gave us, regardless of our circumstances. It's about making the best choices with what we have, and seeking help when needed to break free from unhealthy patterns.

I also know of people who look perfect, but the means they use to achieve those ends can be equally detrimental. I am focusing on the difference between healthy and unhealthy habits—those choices we know in our hearts may not honor the body God gave us, which He calls His temple. I am focusing on health! I empathize deeply because I know how challenging it can be to break free from unhealthy patterns and lower incomes. But I also believe it's possible to heal our relationship with food, and it begins with recognizing if we have an issue and then seeking the support we need to overcome it as best we can.

Why Is This a Real Concern?

An unhealthy relationship with food is not just a physical issue; it affects every aspect of a person's life, including their emotional and spiritual well-being. One man's unhealthy eating habits had him trapped in a cycle of consuming large amounts of junk food, feeling guilty, and then avoiding spiritual practices like prayer because of the shame. However, his emotions improved when he started making healthier choices, and he felt more alive. The new direction highlighted how physical health was directly linked to emotional and spiritual well-being.

Another testimony came from an individual who developed bulimia as a result of depression and unhealthy eating habits. She shared how consuming an entire package of Oreos in one sitting led to feelings of guilt and self-loathing, which spiraled into bulimia to get rid of the food she ate. Her story reflected the inner conflict and shame associated with eating disorders and how these struggles impacted her mental and emotional health. It was only through recognizing the root cause of her behavior and seeking spiritual guidance that she began to heal. She said, "I would eat to the point of feeling sick, and then I'd hate myself for it. The shame was overwhelming, and it drove me further away from God. But when I started to pray and ask God to help me see myself the way He sees me, I began to heal."

The Bible provides clear guidance on the importance of caring for our bodies and avoiding overindulgence. Proverbs 23:20-21 warns us, "Do not join those who drink too much wine or gorge themselves on meat, for drunkards and gluttons become poor, and drowsiness clothes them in rags." This verse emphasizes the dangers of overindulgence and the importance of self-control, a fruit of the Spirit (Galatians 5:22-23).

Wellness: The Importance of Mental and Spiritual Health

What we eat goes beyond food—it's about what we feed our minds. True health encompasses not only physical fitness but also mental well-being. Some of you may have what the world sees as a 'perfect' body, but if your mind consumes negative thoughts or harmful content daily, it's eroding your understanding of how God truly sees you and what you expect from others. While someone with an eating disorder may visibly struggle, mental health battles can remain hidden despite a seemingly healthy exterior. Though I won't delve into every aspect of mental wellness here, I want to underscore its importance. In recent years, the secular world has been at the forefront of mental health discussions due to rising rates of depression and anxiety. While various societal and cultural factors contribute to this trend, Christians are not immune. As an organ, the brain influences our actions, thoughts, beliefs, and daily decisions. Ignoring this reality can have serious consequences. Thus, prioritizing your mental health is as crucial as caring for your body. A better subtitle for the chapter is: we are what we consume. The same principles apply.

We may not have gotten the right messages about our appearance or had healthy practices modeled for us growing up. Still, we can start today by implementing new vocabulary when we talk about our body or the importance we play on appearance to the little people around us watching.

Every morning when my daughter Joy got dressed, my wife Sarah would say to her, "Oh, you look so lovely today. But what's the most important thing?" To which Joy would reply, "What's in my heart?" That message stayed with Joy, who now says it often to her three children.

If we want our children to believe that God designed them to be in "good health" (3 John 1:2) we must also believe this and practice it in our own lives.

The Impact on Witness and Ministry

Poor health can hinder our ability to serve effectively and damage our witness to others. If we can't manage our physical well-being, how can we effectively minister to others or counsel them on spiritual matters? The world's focus on health and wellness makes it critical for Christians to model good stewardship of their bodies and minds, demonstrating the peace and freedom found in Christ through balanced living.

A friend once asked me, "Isn't it interesting that so many health and fitness enthusiasts are nonbelievers? Why do they prioritize long, healthy lives for their families, while many believers seem indifferent?" This observation is quite convicting, especially since, as Christians, we are called to live intentionally, always prepared for the Lord's return (Matthew 24:42). Shouldn't we, of all people, strive to stay healthy and active, not just for our benefit but for the sake of the gospel and the opportunities we have to serve others? When we take control of our health and maintain balance in our diet, exercise, mental health, and rest, we become better equipped to serve our families, communities, and the body of Christ. Moreover, when unbelievers witness Christians exercising self-control and diligence in this area, it is a powerful testimony to the power of Christ in every aspect of life, including our physical well-being.

A story from a famous pastor's life captures this truth vividly. This Bible teacher admitted that he struggled with gluttony in his early years as a pastor. Gluttony is addressed in the Bible and defined in the Merriam-Webster dictionary as "Excess in eating or drinking."[6] Someone candidly told him that taking the pastor's sermons seriously was difficult because of his lack of self-discipline in this area of his life. This pastor was deeply convicted by this honest feedback because, in his words, when he would sit down for a meal, he would "drop my face into the plate and start sucking." He knew his eating habits were out of control and excessive—this eye-opening moment prompted him to make significant changes to his lifestyle, ultimately improving both his physical health and his effectiveness as a witness for Christ.

Practical Applications for Growing in Wellness

Growing in wellness involves taking practical steps in several areas:

diet, spiritual, mental, and emotional health, physical activity, and accountability. Consider the following steps to kickstart growing in wellness. I want to note that it's important to make these changes in manageable ways. Most people gain weight back after fad diets fail because the diet is impossible to maintain beyond the advertised days required to commit. Find small ways to change your lifestyle to keep up for the long term.

Diet and Nutrition: Choosing to eat well is foundational to good health. This means choosing a diet rich in fruits, vegetables, whole grains, and lean proteins while avoiding excessive sugar, unhealthy fats, and processed foods. These changes can transform your physical health, energy levels, mood, and overall quality of life. As 1 Corinthians 10:31 says, "Whether you eat or drink or whatever you do, do it all for the glory of God."

Exercise and Physical Activity: Physical activity is crucial for maintaining health. Whether it's walking, running, or strength training, regular exercise supports not only physical health but also mental and emotional well-being. First Timothy 4:8 acknowledges that "physical training is of some value," while reminding us to prioritize godliness, which is valuable for all things. If physical activity is intimidating, start small: go for a 30-minute walk or ask a friend to try a new workout class in town.

Mental and Emotional Health: Feeding our minds with positive, faith-filled content rather than negativity can profoundly impact our outlook and interactions. One individual shared how they replaced negative media consumption with worship music and uplifting books. "I used to fill my mind with negativity—news, gossip, and criticism. It was no wonder I felt depressed and anxious all the time. One day, I decided to make a change. I started consuming positive, faith-filled content instead. I listened to worship music, read uplifting books, and surrounded myself with encouraging people. Slowly, my mindset shifted. I felt lighter, more hopeful, and more at peace. I realized that what I feed my mind is just as important as what I feed my body." Romans 12:2 reminds us to be transformed by the renewing of our minds so that we can discern God's will. This transformation begins with what we choose to consume mentally and spiritually.

Spiritual Health and Clinging to Truth: My son Jonathan is a clinical psychologist, and I believe therapy is a powerful tool, but we must NOT put it above theology. For example, from a biblical perspective, Jesus and the apostles repeatedly instruct us not to worry or be anxious. In Matthew 6:34, Jesus says, "Therefore do not worry about tomorrow, for tomorrow will worry about itself. Each day has enough trouble of its own." Similarly, Philippians 4:6-7 tells us, "Do not be anxious about anything, but in every situation, by prayer and petition, with thanksgiving, present your requests to God. And the peace of God, which transcends all understanding, will guard your hearts and your minds in Christ Jesus." These are commands to be obeyed immediately, and the word "immediately" gives some people a real problem. Yes, we all know growth is a process, but there is also a need to recognize that when God commands, He expects us to obey in the moment.

This holy tension must be accepted. We must not default to the notion that everything is a process and immediate obedience is impossible.

On a personal note, I know from past seasons when anxiety weighed me down, I lost both energy and my desire to carry on with God's vision for my ministry. At one point, I noticed some hair loss around my forehead, and I realized it was due to the overwhelming stress I was experiencing. Recognizing this, I consciously decided: "I am not going to worry about this anymore." I realized I was imagining worse outcomes than what was happening. As part of making a healthy change, I chose to reframe those circumstances and view them as beneficial. In my case, things weren't as bad as I had imagined, and I needed to speak the truth to my heart rather than fabricate in my mind "what ifs." While it might sound simplistic to suddenly pivot and stop a bad thought process and start a good thought process, this decision is possible and isn't always a shallow proposition. Jesus and the apostles often called people to stop worrying or to put away certain behaviors—it's a decisive moment, a crossroads where one chooses a different path. Many have shared with me how they reached a point where they said, "Enough. I'm done with this." As I reminded myself of unsubstantiated speculations and prayed for God's peace, my stress lessened, and my hair grew back within months! This experience was a tangible reminder of the power of our negative and positive mindset and of faith in God's ability to carry us through difficult times. While it may seem superficial to suggest that someone can stop worrying, it's essential to understand that this decision-making process may entail doing just that! After all, Paul said, "Do not be anxious about anything."

Accountability and Support: Having shared my testimony, I still concur that some things require time. Accountability is a powerful tool for achieving and maintaining wellness. Whether it's through a friend, a counselor, or a support group, having someone to share your struggles with and to hold you accountable can make all the difference. A powerful example of this is an exchange between a pastor and a young woman struggling with a drug addiction. When the pastor suggested making her struggle public to hold her accountable, she realized the power of transparency and the importance of accepting help. True change begins when we step into the light and take the support available - observed behavior changes. James 5:16 encourages us to "confess your sins to each other and pray for each other so that you may be healed." There is healing in confession and in allowing others to help carry our burdens.

Balanced Approach to Health: It's important to approach health holistically, recognizing that physical, emotional, and spiritual well-being are interconnected. Avoid the trap of obsessing over perfection; instead, focus on making balanced, sustainable changes that enhance your quality of life and your ability to serve others.

Testimonies from People Who Have Grown in Wellness

Changing What We Consume: A man shared how his mind was constantly overwhelmed with fear and worry. "I realized it was because I consumed so much negative news and information. Instead, I decided to take control and start my day with God's Word. I also practiced gratitude, listing things I was thankful for each morning. It was like a fog lifting. I felt more hopeful, peaceful, and trusting in God's plan. What I fed my mind changed my whole outlook on life. I didn't become naive about the seriousness of world affairs, but I stopped inundating myself with the repetitive themes of suffering and injustice in the news. I knew these issues persisted, but I recognized that I was carrying a sense of responsibility for changing things beyond my control, and it was wreaking havoc on my soul." Romans 12:2 became his guiding verse: "Do not conform to the pattern of this world, but be transformed by the renewing of your mind."

How Forgiveness Aids Our Health: A man shared how his physical health improved after he forgave those who had hurt him. He had been holding onto bitterness and resentment, which manifested in physical ailments and stress. "I was constantly anxious, and my body felt the effects—headaches, fatigue, and even hair loss. When I finally chose to forgive and let go, I experienced emotional freedom and a remarkable improvement in my physical health. It was as if a weight had been lifted off my shoulders." His story reflects the wisdom of Proverbs 17:22, which says, "A cheerful heart is good medicine, but a crushed spirit dries up the bones."

Overcoming the Cycle of Guilt and Shame: A woman shared how she used to dwell on her past mistakes, constantly feeding herself guilt and shame. "It was exhausting and kept me stuck in a cycle of self-condemnation. One day, I decided to change my inner dialogue. I started reading scriptures about God's forgiveness and grace. I began declaring them over myself, refusing to let the enemy's lies consume me. I found freedom in the truth of who I am in Christ—a new creation, redeemed and set free. I now live in victory, no longer defined by my past but by God's grace and love." Her testimony is a powerful example of 2 Corinthians 5:17, which says, "If anyone is in Christ, the new creation has come: The old has gone, the new is here!"

Breaking the Cycle of Toxic Relationships: A woman described how she realized that her friendships were toxic and filled with gossip and negativity. "I was becoming just like the people I spent time with—negative, judgmental, and bitter. I knew I had to make a change, but it was hard to distance myself from people I'd known for so long. I started praying for wisdom and courage, and God brought new, positive influences into my life. Now, I have friendships that encourage growth and faith, and I'm a much happier person because of it." Her journey reflects Proverbs 13:20: "Walk with the wise and become wise, for a companion of fools suffers harm."

The Power of Accountability: A woman who had struggled with weight loss shared how she finally found victory by opening up to a trusted friend. She accepted the challenge to "do something" about her health and sought nutrition counseling. She was held accountable for everything she ate and changed her lifestyle, her relationship with food, and her attitude toward exercise. She said, "I realized that I couldn't do it alone. I needed someone to hold me accountable, to encourage me, and to challenge me when I was tempted to give up. I started tracking everything I ate and worked on being mindful of my choices. Over time, the weight came off, but more importantly, I felt empowered and closer to God. I began every morning with prayer and Scripture, and He gave me the strength to make healthier choices."

Finding Joy in Healthy Living: A man shared how he had always viewed exercise as a chore until he experienced a health scare that made him reevaluate his lifestyle. He began incorporating daily exercise and healthier eating habits, and to his surprise, he found a new sense of joy and vitality. "I used to dread going to the gym, but now I see it as a way to take care of the body God has given me. I feel stronger, more energetic, and more alive. It's not just about looking better; it's about feeling better and serving others more effectively." His testimony is a reminder of 1 Corinthians 6:20: "You were bought at a price. Therefore honor God with your bodies."

Balancing Physical and Spiritual Discipline: An older woman shared how, after years of neglecting her health, she prioritized physical and spiritual discipline. "I joined a walking group at my church and started participating in a Bible study. The combination of physical activity and spiritual growth was transformative. I felt more energetic, focused, and connected to God. I realized that caring for my body is part of my worship." Her story reflects the holistic approach to wellness found in 1 Timothy 4:8, which teaches that physical training is valuable, but godliness is even more important.

The testimonies shared in this chapter highlight the profound impact that good stewardship of our physical and mental health can have on every aspect of our lives. "You are what you eat" is more than just a saying—it's a reminder that everything we consume, physically and mentally, shapes who we are. By intentionally caring for our bodies and minds, we honor God and equip ourselves to serve Him and others more effectively.

The Bible calls us to be good stewards of all God has given us, including our health. Whether it's through diet, exercise, mental focus, or emotional healing, each step we take toward wellness is a step toward fulfilling the purpose God has for us. As 3 John 1:2 says, "Dear friend, I pray that you may enjoy good health and that all may go well with you, even as your soul is getting along well." Sarah and I have made this prayer our own for decades. May we all strive to grow in wellness, knowing that we reflect God's goodness and grace to a watching world as we do.

TWELVE

Restoration
(You Cannot Pour From an Empty Cup)

Regular reflection and restoration are essential for spiritual and emotional growth. Being still before the Lord restores our minds and hearts, equipping us to grow and pour into others' lives. Rest is not a luxury but a necessity for maintaining health. When Christians become too busy to pause, reflect, and rest, they risk their well-being, the health of their relationships, and the strength of their testimony. When we incorporate rest into our weekly schedules, we are more energized and prepared for difficult moments—the difficult conversations, disappointing news, and unmet expectations.

As Psalm 46:10 says, "Be still, and know that I am God." Taking time to be still before God renews our spirit, enabling us to serve as more effective witnesses. In this stillness, we gain clarity,

Taking time to
be still before
God renews
our spirit,
enabling us
to serve as
more effective
witnesses.

strength, and the wisdom to navigate life's demands gracefully and purposefully.

Christians Showing the Secular World the Importance of the Sabbath

The Bible calls us to rest and reflect, recognizing that "You cannot pour from an empty cup." This principle in the health and wellness space might be called "self-care," and many businesses are adopting sabbaticals or work environments that ensure their staff is not burned out.

The "Sabbath in business" principle has been exemplified by businesses like Chick-fil-A, which closed its doors on Sundays since its beginning in 1946.[7] Despite criticism, this practice highlights the profound value of setting aside time for restoration. Exodus 20:8-10 commands, "Remember the Sabbath day, to keep it holy. Six days you shall labor and do all your work, but the seventh day is a Sabbath to the Lord your God. On it you shall not do any work." A day of rest revitalizes us, like recharging our spiritual batteries, allowing us to step back and reflect on God's handiwork. It's not about idleness but about experiencing joy and delight in His presence, engaging in meaningful conversations, laughing deeply, discussing serious ideas, and connecting intimately with the Lord.

As a business, Chick-fil-A has a mission statement that echoes the biblical principle. "Closing our business on Sunday, the Lord's

Day, is our way of honoring God and showing our loyalty. We believe this is the best way to maintain a healthy balance between work and worship, as well as rest and reflection for our employees and their families."[8]

While some might see this decision as a loss of revenue, it has proven to be a source of strength for the company, affirming founder Truett Cathy's belief that, "We aren't in the chicken business; we're in the people business." (And let's not forget what we learned about generosity in the Stewardship chapter about the paradox that those who give receive!) This commitment to rest and worship, even at the potential cost of profit, which has not hurt their bottom line, underscores the truth that true success comes from obedience to God, not merely worldly gain.

Who Is Foolish, And What Is Futile?

Ecclesiastes 2:22-23 (NIV) reflects on the futility and weariness of relentless labor: "What do people get for all the toil and anxious striving with which they labor under the sun? All their days their work is grief and pain; even at night their minds do not rest. This too is meaningless." This passage warns against overwork and the neglect of rest, highlighting the importance of balancing labor with spiritual renewal.

A life consumed by work without a higher purpose will lead to emptiness. Ecclesiastes warns against the pursuit of endless toil. The writer of Ecclesiastes reflects on the weariness that comes from striving for success or achievement, only to find that it does not bring lasting fulfillment. Ecclesiastes reminds us to seek balance and to find purpose beyond an obsessive compulsion to narrowly pursue a single course to the neglect of God and His purpose and pleasure.

This doesn't just apply to the husband working long hours to prove his worth to his boss but also to the countless women who have bought into the lie that they must do it all at once to prove they are strong and independent. The truth is, no one can do it all at once.

Many of us fall short in achieving restoration by prioritizing work or ministry over personal well-being and family. This misplaced focus can lead to self-imposed stress and burnout. Some act like "workaholics" described in Ecclesiastes, where the pursuit of success becomes an endless cycle of toil and anxiety, leaving them empty and unfulfilled. The Bible warns that such labor is "meaningless" when it detracts from our relationship with God and others.

How Ignoring Routine Restoration Can Harm Ourselves and Those Around Us

A Father's Confession: A father admitted that he frequently used the excuse of being "stressed out" to avoid taking on more responsibilities at home. He confessed, "I would come home and collapse into my chair, claiming to be drained. But the truth is,

I was avoiding my family. I used 'stress' as a shield to keep my wife and kids from asking more of me. It was easier to claim exhaustion than to face the reality that I wasn't finding joy in my relationship with Christ." He realized that his stress was not just about work; it was about a deeper spiritual emptiness. Convicted, he turned back to Christ, seeking true peace and purpose.

A Woman's Awakening: A woman shared how she constantly complained about being overwhelmed and stressed to everyone around her. "I would start every conversation with, 'I'm just so stressed,' hoping people would sympathize with me. But deep down, I knew I was using stress as an excuse. I had a stress story to tell, and I told it to solicit empathy. I felt energized by venting to others. But the Lord convicted me of my self-centeredness, negativity, and complaints. I realized that constantly dwelling on my stress wasn't helping me or anyone around me. It was only perpetuating a cycle of negativity. I began to pray for a spirit of gratitude and intentionally focus on my life's blessings rather than the burdens. Slowly, my mindset shifted. Instead of using stress as my default narrative, I began speaking life and truth into my situations. I found peace by trusting God more deeply, and the need for sympathy from others faded as I experienced His grace in a new way."

A Pastor's Recovery from Burnout: A pastor described how his relentless pursuit of ministry success left him spiritually and emotionally depleted. "I thought I was doing it all for God, but in reality, I was doing it for recognition and approval.

I became so busy serving others that I forgot to serve my soul." He recognized that he could not effectively serve his congregation in this state, so he took a sabbatical to reconnect with God and his family. "During that time away, I realized how far I had drifted from my first love, Jesus. I started each day with prayer and Scripture, not because I had to prepare a sermon, but because I needed it for myself." This time of restoration not only healed him but also revitalized his ministry. "Now, I minister out of the overflow of what God is doing in me, not out of my empty reserves."

Misplaced Priorities: A man confessed that he had placed his career above his family, believing he was doing it for their benefit. "I thought working long hours and earning more money would make me a good provider. But in the end, all my kids wanted was my time, and all I gave them was absence." He realized that the grief and pain from his relentless work hours had eroded his relationship with his children. This emotional toll was a stark realization that his work, which he thought was meaningful, felt "meaningless" in the light of lost family time. "I had to learn the hard way that work doesn't mean success at home. I had to re-prioritize and put my family and faith back where they belong."

The "Totaled Woman" Phenomenon: Years ago, the book *Total Woman* topped the bestseller lists, captivating many. However, I have termed this phenomenon the "Totaled Woman." I describe how some women, in their attempt to balance full-time work and family life, feel completely exhausted and drained—the "Totaled

Woman." Like a crashed car is totaled, these women hit a wall with the pedal to the metal. "I felt like I had to be perfect at everything—at work, home, and even church. But the more I tried to hold it all together, the more I fell apart." This occurs when they try to fulfill every role perfectly, often neglecting their own needs and the deeper emotional needs of their children and spouse. This leads to a feeling of constantly giving the "leftovers" of their energy and attention to their families, causing both physical and emotional fatigue. "I would get home and have nothing left to give. I was running on empty and it showed. My kids were getting the worst of me, not the best. I knew something had to change."

What the Scripture Says on Being Restored

The Bible teaches that true restoration is found in abiding deeply in Christ and living out His principles daily. This restoration is not just about physical rest but a holistic renewal that touches the mind, body, and spirit.

Abiding in Christ: Jesus emphasizes the importance of remaining connected to Him in John 15:4-5: "Remain in me, as I also remain in you. No branch can bear fruit by itself; it must remain in the vine. Neither can you bear fruit unless you remain in me." This passage reveals that true fruitfulness and strength come from a deep, abiding relationship with Christ. It's more than just believing in Him; it's about being nourished by His presence, drawing strength and purpose from Him daily.

Practicing Sabbath Rest: The Sabbath is not merely a day off but a divine command for rest and reflection. Exodus 20:8-10 instructs, "Remember the Sabbath day, to keep it holy. Six days you shall labor and do all your work, but the seventh day is a Sabbath to the Lord your God. On it you shall not do any work." It's an invitation to reset our focus, recognizing that our value comes from who we are in Him, not from our productivity.

Following Jesus' Example: Jesus Himself modeled the importance of solitude and prayer. Mark 1:35 records, "Very early in the morning, while it was still dark, Jesus got up, left the house and went off to a solitary place, where he prayed." In the midst of His demanding ministry, Jesus often withdrew to be alone with the Father, showing us that even in the busiest seasons, making time for quiet reflection is essential for maintaining spiritual vitality.

Making Melody in Your Heart: Paul encourages believers in Ephesians 5:19 and Colossians 3:16 to "speak to one another with psalms, hymns, and spiritual songs. Sing and make music in your heart to the Lord." This isn't just about singing; it's about cultivating an attitude of gratitude and worship that permeates every aspect of our lives.

Casting All Anxieties on Him: 1 Peter 5:7 reminds us to "Cast all your anxiety on Him because He cares for you." Restoration begins when we surrender our worries and burdens to Christ, acknowledging that He is in control and we are not.

Renewing Our Minds: Romans 12:2 calls us to "be transformed by the renewing of your mind." This renewal comes through immersing ourselves in God's Word, allowing His truths to reshape our thoughts and attitudes.

Restoration, then, is not simply about taking breaks or managing stress. It's a radical reorientation of our lives toward God, where we find our identity, purpose, and strength in Him. It's about moving from a place of striving to a place of abiding.

Testimonies on How We Can Find Restoration

Brother Lawrence's Practice of Continuous Communion: Brother Lawrence, a 17th-century monk, exemplified the practice of maintaining a constant dialogue with God. Despite his humble role as a kitchen worker, he engaged in an ongoing conversation with God, transforming mundane tasks into acts of worship. He prayed, "O my God, since Thou art with me, and I must now, in obedience to Thy commands, apply my mind to these outward things, I beseech Thee to grant me the grace to continue in Thy presence; and to this end, do Thou prosper me with Thy assistance, receive all my works, and possess all my affections."[9] This continuous communion helped Brother Lawrence find a sense of peace and purpose, even in the midst of his daily chores. He maintained that his sense of God's presence was often stronger during his work than in formal worship settings, underscoring the potential for finding God in every moment. His life teaches us that true peace and purpose are not

His [Brother Lawrence]
life teaches us that true
peace and purpose are
not found in escaping
the busyness of life,
but in embracing each
moment as an opportunity
to connect with God.

found in escaping the busyness of life, but in embracing each moment as an opportunity to connect with God.

Mission Project Testimony: During a mission project in Mississippi, an elderly African-American woman who had been indentured as a young girl shared her story. She spent her life laboring in the scorching cotton fields. I asked her how she survived those grueling years. She responded, "Each morning I'd awaken before dawn. The day before me would be another day of drudgery in the cotton fields. To make it through the heat and humidity I'd ask the Lord to give me a song for the day. If I had a song, I could hum and sing it while picking cotton. Faithfully, He'd give me a song. Each day I'd sing to Him and find comfort in His presence." Her story is a powerful testimony of finding strength, joy, and divine companionship through a simple yet profound act of worship, transforming her arduous labor into a daily communion with God. This echoes Paul's words to the Ephesians and Colossians, where he encourages believers to "speak to one another with psalms, hymns, and songs from the Spirit. Sing and make music from your heart to the Lord" (Ephesians 5:19) and to "let the message of Christ dwell among you richly... singing to God with gratitude in your hearts" (Colossians 3:16).

Eric Liddell's Commitment to Sabbath Rest: Eric Liddell, an Olympic runner renowned for his unwavering commitment to Sabbath rest, refused to compete on Sundays, as depicted in the movie *Chariots of Fire*. Despite societal and professional pressure, he prioritized his obedience to God's principles over the prospect of winning a gold medal. Reflecting on his decision, Liddell said, "I believe God made me for a purpose, but He also made me fast. And when I run, I feel His pleasure." His refusal to run on Sunday was met with criticism and disbelief, yet Liddell remained firm in his faith. God honored his obedience when a fellow runner offered to switch events, allowing Liddell to run in the 400 meters instead of the 100 meters. Against all odds, he won the gold medal. His story is a powerful testimony of how honoring God's commandments brings true fulfillment and blessing. As believers have affirmed through the ages, "Those who honor Me I will honor" (1 Samuel 2:30).

Practical Applications for Being Restored

Prioritize Quiet Time with God: Start your day in stillness before the Lord. Make time to sit with Him in prayer, meditation, or reflection. Psalm 46:10 says, "Be still, and know that I am God." By doing this, you allow God to restore your mind, heart, and spirit, and you'll be better equipped to face the day with peace and strength.

I often hear this kind of testimony. "For years, I started my mornings in a whirlwind—rushing to get the kids ready, checking emails, and grabbing coffee on the go. I was constantly overwhelmed and felt disconnected, not only from my family but also from God. One day, after a particularly stressful morning that ended in tears and frustration, a friend gently suggested that I carve out a few minutes each morning for quiet time with the

Lord. I remember thinking, 'I don't have time for that!' But I was desperate for change, so I decided to try it. I began waking up just 15 minutes earlier. I'd sit in the stillness of my living room, the house dark and quiet, and simply read a few verses of Scripture, letting Psalm 46:10—"Be still, and know that I am God"— sink deep into my spirit. At first, it felt awkward and forced. I wasn't used to just being still. But over time, those few minutes became my lifeline. I found that God wasn't just a part of my day; He was the source of my strength for everything I faced. Now, that quiet time is non-negotiable. It's where I meet God, where He speaks to my heart, and where I am reminded that He is in control, no matter how chaotic life gets."

Set Boundaries Around Your Time: Reflect on whether you are overcommitting yourself to work, activities, or even ministry. Are you so busy that your time with loved ones or God is being compromised? Set healthy boundaries and guard your time for rest, family, and personal renewal.

I love the story of Susanna Wesley, the mother of John and Charles Wesley. She was known for her devotion to prayer. Despite the challenges she faced as a wife and mother of 10 children, she prioritized her relationship with God. When she needed a quiet moment to pray, she would tie her apron over her head, signaling to her family that she was unavailable for conversation or distraction. We need to let this humorous but true story remind us that setting a boundary is okay!

Seek Balance, Not Perfection: You don't have to have everything under control at all times. The goal is not perfection but balance. Learn to say no when necessary, and understand that your well-being is just as important as your responsibilities to others.

When we had young kids, Sarah felt guilty that she did not have a consistent devotional time due to interruptions of three young children. I understood but said, "It's okay. This is a season that will pass, and you will have a lot more time when they are older, and you'll feel more balanced." Looking back after 50 years of marriage, the last three decades have found her having a ton of quiet time in a meaningful and balanced way. Yes, she felt guilty in that she should be doing better in her quiet times with Jesus with toddlers, and that she could be less imperfect. No real debate there, but the Lord understands and is forgiving. In that sense, Sarah made up for lost time!

Be Mindful of Your Emotional Energy: Like the wife who wrote to me, many of us are pouring out all day, leaving nothing for those who matter most, including our spouses and families. Make sure that you are not draining yourself by overextending in relationships or work without replenishing your own emotional reserves.

I once received an email from a wife whose message resonated deeply with this theme of depletion. She shared: "My husband tries hard and makes many emotional deposits. But my coworkers, our kids, and others I encounter each day make so many withdrawals. I end up empty at the end of the day. It seems unfair to my husband that he tries so hard, but others sap my emotional energy away, leaving me stressed and unhappy. I don't want to lack emotional resilience, but I am truly exhausted and running on fumes. He deserves my best, but there's just not much left of me by the time he gets home." Her transparency reveals a cry for help and the need for wisdom to do things differently. Like many of us, she is emotionally drained, stressed, and burnt out. Her story is a reminder that we cannot give what we do not have, and this includes emotional availability, patience, and joy. When Christians live in a constant state of depletion, our relationships and witness are affected. When unbelievers observe this, they see someone who is struggling rather than a reflection of Christ's peace.

Practice the Presence of God: We can't expect to just automatically know how to incorporate restoration into our lives. This may be something we need to practice. Start with something small—five minutes a day in prayer or meditating on Scriptures while on a walk. Gradually increase your time, or invite God into moments you hadn't previously—a busy commute, a stressful meeting, or doing house chores. When we practice in small ways, we build a habit and prepare our minds for where to turn when facing something much more daunting.

"As I immersed myself in work and serving others, I neglected my own spiritual needs and the presence of God in my daily life. Brother Lawrence's example showed me that in the busiest moments, it's crucial to keep our minds and hearts connected to God, transforming every mundane task into an act of worship."

Howard Rutledge, a POW in Vietnam, endured harsh conditions but found strength in memorized Scripture and hymns. He shared how these spiritual practices sustained him during nearly seven years of imprisonment, including five years in solitary confinement. Reflecting on this, Rutledge said, "I would pray, hum hymns silently, quote Scripture, and think about what that verse meant to me…the enemy knew that the best way to break a man's resistance was to crush his spirit in a lonely cell." The former POW states, "Scripture and hymns might be boring to some, but it was the way we conquered our enemy and overcame the power of death around us."[10]

Acknowledge When You Need Help: If you are consistently running on empty, it may be time to seek wisdom or assistance. Whether through counseling, support groups, or simply talking to a friend, recognize when you need restoration and allow others to help you find balance.

Personal holiness is largely a solitary enterprise. The inward disciplines of meditation, prayer, and study. We can know this but not act on it. A famous pastor said that we can only become an authentic Christian from solitude, not on a steady diet of activity. Years later he morally fell, losing everything he worked so hard to achieve. He did not acknowledge he needed help.

Restoration through rest and reflection is essential for our well-being and spiritual health. It allows us to serve more effectively and live lives that reflect the peace and purpose found in Christ.

By taking the time to be still before God, setting boundaries, and seeking balance, we can experience the true renewal that comes from abiding in Him. As seen through the testimonies shared, those who prioritize restoration find strength, joy, and deeper relationships with God and others, ultimately becoming better witnesses of His love and grace.

Live in a way that reflects the character of Christ, just as an athlete competes at the highest level to reflect their dedication and skill. It's about setting the bar high in our spiritual lives and striving to clear it, no matter the cost.

Conclusion

Should we live above the bar in these twelve areas? Yes, that's the challenge and the goal and it is a worthy aim. But these twelve must be seen in the context of a larger calling that I have not even addressed in this book. I surface them here as a reminder that the bar on these 12 are not all extraordinary, but what the world expects of us and of themselves. Really living "above the bar" means striving to reach an even higher standard.

Turn the Other Cheek: "If anyone slaps you on the right cheek, turn to them the other cheek also" (Matthew 5:39). This means choosing not to retaliate when wronged. It's about having the strength to rise above the natural response of revenge and instead respond with grace and patience.

Go the Extra Mile: "If anyone forces you to go one mile, go with them two miles" (Matthew 5:41). This calls us to exceed what is required or expected. It's like an athlete pushing beyond their limits, not for recognition, but to show generosity and a willingness to serve others.

Love Your Enemies: "But I tell you, love your enemies and pray for those who persecute you" (Matthew 5:44). Loving those who oppose or hurt us is challenging, much like striving for a personal best in competition. It requires inner strength, discipline, and a deep commitment to living by love, even when it's difficult.

Give to the One Who Asks: "Give to the one who asks you, and do not turn away from the one who wants to borrow from you" (Matthew 5:42). This principle teaches generosity without expecting anything in return. It's like an athlete giving their all in every performance, regardless of whether they win or lose.

Bless Those Who Curse You: "Bless those who curse you, pray for those who mistreat you" (Luke 6:28). Instead of responding with anger or resentment, we are called to respond with kindness and prayer. It's the emotional equivalent of maintaining composure and sportsmanship even when the game gets tough.

Forgive Seventy Times Seven: "I tell you, not seven times, but seventy-seven times" (Matthew 18:22). Forgiveness is a discipline that must be practiced continually, just like an athlete trains daily.

It's about letting go of grudges and offenses again and again, striving to maintain peace and compassion.

Do Good to Those Who Hate You: "Do good to those who hate you" (Luke 6:27). Choosing to do good to those who wish you harm is the ultimate test of character, akin to competing in the toughest event. It's about rising above personal hurt and choosing to act with integrity and love.

Each of these teachings is a call to rise above the ordinary, to live in a way that reflects the character of Christ, just as an athlete competes at the highest level to reflect their dedication and skill. It's about setting the bar high in our spiritual lives and striving to clear it, no matter the cost.

By contrast then, this book should be a piece of cake! As Christ-followers, we should find it easier to demonstrate:

Emotional Intelligence (Keep Your Cool)

Resilience (Bounce Back Stronger)

Stewardship in Finances (A Penny Saved Is a Penny Earned)

Valuing Time (Time Is Money)

Originality in Problem-Solving (Think Outside the Box)

Education for a Lifetime (You're Never Too Old to Learn)

Work Ethic (Rome Wasn't Built in a Day)

Adaptability (Bend but Do Not Break)

Communication Skills (It's Not What You Say, It's How You Say It)

Authenticity (Honesty Is the Best Policy)

Growth in Wellness (You Are What You Eat)

Restoration (You Cannot Pour From an Empty Cup)

These twelve qualities set the bar, and when we showcase these, we win hearts, influence lives, and appeal to the world. We are in this together, so let's pray for one another to this end. In our deepest hearts, all of us want to make a difference for Christ and His Kingdom.

Notes

Letter From Emerson

1. CMS Admin. "Revivals in the Camp - Christianity Today." Christianity Today, 1992, www.christianitytoday.com/1992/01/revivals-in-camp/.

Chapter 3: Stewardship in Finances (A Penny Saved Is a Penny Earned)

2. Arthur C. Brooks, "Why Giving Matters," Y Magazine, Summer 2009, https://magazine.byu.edu/article/why-giving-matters/.

Chapter 5: Originality in Problem-Solving (Think Outside the Box)

3. "Home," Dream Center, Accessed on September 29, 2024, https://www.dreamcenter.org/

Chapter 6: Education for a Lifetime (You're Never Too Old to Learn)

4. Adam Winters, "The Real Colonel Sanders and His Surprising Ties to Southern Seminary." Towers, Southern Equip, November 2015, https://equip.sbts.edu/publications/towers/the-real-colonel-sanders-and-his-surprising-ties-to-southern-seminary/.

Chapter 9: Communication Skills (It's Not What You Say, It's How You Say It)

5. Ellison, Mark D. 2019. "Family, Marriage, and Celibacy in the New Testament." Edited by Lincoln H. Blumell. New Testament History, Culture, and Society: A Background to the Texts of the New Testament, May. https://rsc.byu.edu/new-testament-history-culture-society/family-marriage-celibacy-new-testament.

Chapter 11: Growth in Wellness (You Are What You Eat)

6. "Gluttony," Merriam-Webster, accessed September 26, 2024, https://www.merriam-webster.com/dictionary/gluttony.

Chapter 12: Restoration (You Cannot Pour From an Empty Cup)

7. "Why is Chick-fil-A Closed on Sunday?" Chick-fil-A, accessed September 26, 2024, https://www.chick-fil-a.com/customer-support/who-we-are/our-culture-and-values/why-is-chick-fil-a-closed-on-sunday#:~:tet=Our%20founder%20S.

8. Truett Cathy, Eat Mor Chikin, Inspire More People: Doing Business the Chick-fil-A Way (Looking Glass Books, 2002).

9. Brother Lawrence, The Practice of the Presence of God. (Martino Fine Books, 2016).

10. Jan White, "Veteran Told About His Experiences in Hanoi Hilton," The Andalusia Star News, November 2023. https://www.andalusiastarnews.com/2023/11/12/column-veteran-told-about-his-experiences-in-hanoi-hilton/

Love and Respect Ministries

Join our communities on Facebook, Instagram and TikTok:
@loverespectinc

For podcasts, articles, videos, online courses,
books and church resources find us at:
loveandrespect.com

About the Author

Dr. Emerson Eggerichs is an internationally known author and speaker on the topics of marriage, parenting, communication and more. Based on five decades of counseling as well as scientific and biblical research, he founded Love and Respect Ministries with his wife Sarah in 1999, which is actively impacting countless relationships all over the world.

Dr. Eggerichs has spoken to owners, coaches, players and spouses in the NFL, PGA and NBA. He has keynoted at national business events, professional counseling conventions and more. He's addressed universities, mega churches, the U.S. military, CEO groups, and the poorest of the poor in India.

Getting his undergraduate and graduate degrees at Wheaton College he went on to receive a Masters of Divinity from Dubuque Seminary, and holds a Ph.D. in Child and Family Ecology from Michigan State University. He has authored several books, including the New York Times bestseller *Love & Respect* which has sold over 2 million copies.

Prior to launching the Love and Respect Conferences, Dr. Eggerichs was the senior pastor of East Lansing Trinity Church for nearly 20 years. He and Sarah have been married since 1973 and have three adult children, and seven grandchildren.

Made in the USA
Monee, IL
10 June 2026

52190823R00121